J. Graham

Savigear's Guide to Horsemanship and Horse Traning

J. Graham

Savigear's Guide to Horsemanship and Horse Traning

ISBN/EAN: 9783337313906

Printed in Europe, USA, Canada, Australia, Japan

Cover: Foto ©Andreas Hilbeck / pixelio.de

More available books at **www.hansebooks.com**

SAVIGEAR'S RIDING SCHOOL

Earls Court,

London, S.W.

Telegraphic Address :—

"SAVIGEAR, EARLS COURT"

MILITARY CLASSES
FOR
OFFICERS AND ARMY CANDIDATES.

Late Chief Riding Instructor to

R.M. COLLEGE.   STAFF COLLEGE.   R.H.A   17th LANCERS

EQUITATION ACCORDING TO THE BOOK OF AIDS.

Long, High and Buck Jumps Taught. Water Jumps. Polo. Pig Sticking. Tilting at the Ring. Picking up Stirrup Iron with hand and lance, &c.

Dismounting and Mounting at a Gallop, etc.

SEPARATE CLASSES FOR LADIES.

Chargers and Ladies' Horses Trained.

10, 12, 14 & 16,
Earl's Court Square.

Dr. MILLER MAGUIRE begs to state that he requests all his pupils to join the Riding Class. He knows that this class has the approval of the Military Authorities, and commends itself to all experienced officers.

Every Militia Officer and every Candidate for Woolwich or Sandhurst would find it a great advantage to his career, besides giving him the best exercise that a student can have.

JOHN A. SEAVERNS

SAVIGEAR'S GUIDE

TO

HORSEMANSHIP

AND

HORSE TRAINING

EDITED BY

LIEUT-COL. J. GRAHAM.

ALL RIGHTS RESERVED.

LONDON:
FARMER & SONS, KENSINGTON,
AND SOLD AT THE EARL'S COURT RIDING SCHOOL.
1899.

PREFACE.

Perhaps the reader will pardon a word of explanation as to the origin and objects of this Guide.

Having passed through an Army riding school, and been afterwards employed for three years in superintending the military equitation of Students preparing for the Army, I naturally felt interested on hearing that Mr. Savigear, the well-known Instructor from Sandhurst, had opened a riding school at Earl's Court. Having further ascertained that Army Tutors in the neighbourhood regarded Mr. Savigear's establishment as a boon to the candidates under their care, I became a frequent visitor at the School.

During my visits I have been impressed with the excellence of Mr. Savigear's methods and with the rapid progress made by his pupils. This result is doubtless due in part to his exceptional experience as an Instructor for a period of nearly forty years, first in the Royal Horse Artillery, next in the 17th Lancers, and afterwards at the Royal Military College. The fact should also be mentioned that he was the first promoter of the Islington Tournament and assisted at its earliest meetings.

Mr. Savigear's patience and kindness in dealing both with men and horses are notable features of his system and have certainly contributed to his success, while the information which he is able to communicate on everything connected with riding makes him a very interesting mentor.

Such are some of the considerations which induced me to suggest the preparation of a manual embracing, in small compass, the practical course of instruction pursued at the Earl's Court School, and giving details that might be helpful to all in the riding and general management of the horse.

It is hoped that officers and candidates who have passed through a course of instruction and wish to keep up their riding, will find the book useful as a guide, that it will help them to direct soldiers and grooms, and diminish the number of cruel and expensive mistakes constantly occurring in connection with the horse's treatment.

J. GRAHAM.

March, 1899.

CONTENTS.

1. INTRODUCTION 9
2. RIDING SCHOOL EXERCISES ... 12
3. MILITARY EQUITATION 18
4. LADIES' EQUITATION 82
5. THE TRAINING OF HORSES 96
6. SADDLES 116
7. DRIVING 120
8. STABLES AND OTHER SUBJECTS 127

Horsemanship & Horse Training

INTRODUCTION.

It is assumed that the Army system of equitation, when well and patiently expounded, is the best foundation for horsemanship, whether military or civil. In fact, "The Book of Aids" may be regarded as an unrivalled guide to the acquisition of good hands and seat. It is therefore reproduced here with sufficient fulness for the instruction of officers, who, if they learn the following lessons satisfactorily, may rest assured that no one will challenge their proficiency as horsemen. Non-military pupils, by going through the same course, will attain a firmness of seat and a lightness of hand, which nothing else can give them.

It is a mistake to suppose that a hunting seat, as it is called, is essentially different from a military seat. Both are exactly in the same place, namely, on the part of the horse's back where there is least motion, and where nature intends the weight to be carried. The positions of the riders' hands and feet are different in their respective cases, as will be hereafter explained, but for purposes of instruction the actual seats are identical. It is therefore very strongly held that, for whatever kind of riding a pupil may be preparing, his best and surest course is to pass carefully through the regulation exercises, and thus lay what has already been described as the best foundation.

Ladies too, should be taught these exercises, for no other system will give them the same mastery over their horses, or the same gracefulness and safety on horseback. If a lady be sent out to ride without having been perfectly instructed in the use of the aids, and without the practice which cannot well be obtained except in a good riding school, she is placed in a position of danger, and the risk is still greater if there be any uncertainty about the training of her horse. The advice given on the training of horses, driving, stables, and other matters, is based on experience, and will be found trustworthy. It is intended to furnish those who have finished a course of riding, with facts and ideas which will be useful to them as owners of horses, for it is not enough to learn the mechanical business of sitting on and directing a horse; the horseman should sympathize with his four-footed servant, and should be acquainted with the best modes of treating him. He should also have some knowledge of horse-breaking, and insist, whenever he has the authority to do so, on its being carried out in a kind and reasonable way.

RIDING SCHOOL EXERCISES.

It is not to be expected that anyone can ride well without having been systematically taught, and without having remained long enough under instruction to become thoroughly familiar with the system followed. In this country the army system may be considered the best for all practical purposes, and, as already stated, it has been made the basis of the school instructions in this manual, subject to modification when necessary.

Some people on the continent still cultivate the ancient and elaborate horsemanship, once so much admired as the result of the highest training in horse and man, but generally deemed by our countrymen to be too theatrical and ornate. Movements like the *piaffe* and *croupade* have been relegated to the arena, and the tendency now is to make our riding exercises more simple and practical. Even in our army riding-schools the drill has recently been simplified, not that higher training is useless, but that it takes up so much time for which it offers no sufficient advantages. A few hunting men affect to despise school riding altogether, but this is going to an extreme, and can only be taken as an evidence of ignorance.

Between the *piaffe* and *croupade* idea and that of the cross-country rider who is ignorant of aids, a safe and sure place is claimed for the present system. It certainly supplies instruction preparatory alike to military, cross-country, and Park riding. Very little explanation is required to show that the difference between them is non-essential, while in all the main points the similarity is absolute. A hunting man makes himself comfortable by pushing his feet home in his stirrups, he can use both hands on his reins, he does not usually carry himself very erect, and he lets his horse extend himself and walk with his head low. This is all quite consistent with what the horse and his rider have to do. The soldier, on the other hand, can use only one hand for his reins, and must keep his horse collected, so as promptly to change his direction; he must hold his own body and head erect, not only for the sake of perfect balance, but in order to use his weapons effectively. This is also reasonable and necessary. But in both cases, and in that of the Park rider, which is their connecting link, the man is, or ought to be, placed on the same part of the horse's back, and should produce the same effects on the horse's mouth. In all cases he ought to have begun by acquiring balance, in order to obviate hanging on his horse's mouth, and likewise in all cases, he ought to know the application of the leg which saves and assists the horse, and causes him to move in a desired direction when no other means are effectual.

Now, it is quite evident, and is often remarked by those who know what horsemanship is, that the riding in the Park is not what it ought to be in the capital of a country professing the greatest horse-knowledge, and possessing the best horses in the world. Riding-masters, so called, are often to be seen there with their pupils, but they generally give an exhibition of "how not to do it," allowing their charges to pound along anyhow, and to display, without correction, nearly every fault of which a person on horseback can be guilty. Of course it is better to correct mistakes in private than in public, but it seems unusual to do so at all. Those who will take the trouble to inquire will find that in the majority of civilian riding schools the pupils practise riding, it is true, but receive little or no instruction.

It has repeatedly been suggested, and not without good reason, that riding-masters should be subjected to an examination before being permitted to practise their calling. Life and limb may be sacrificed in consequence of employing an inefficient riding-master, but the worst of the class is preferable to a coachman or groom. Servants such as these, however good and honest, are, in nearly every instance, utterly incapable of teaching.

Even if they are themselves able to ride, which is very seldom the case, owing to their heavy hands, they do so less as reasoning beings than from a kind of instinct or habit; they have no power of imparting knowledge, and are immediately out of their depth when confronted with a " why and wherefore."

It certainly is desirable that an exercise so healthful and agreeable as riding, should be learned in the best possible way, not only for the sake of the rider, but also on account of the horse. The comfort of both is promoted by the lightness of the rider's hand and the proper position of his body and legs. If the horse could only speak he would remonstrate against the cruel manner in which his mouth is hurt by the bit, when badly taught men haul heavily or onesidedly at the reins. He would likewise complain of the heavy heels that kick his sides, and of the uncouth means employed to start or stop him. These and similar matters should be thought of by all riders, and even if they consider themselves tolerably experienced, they would probably derive advantage from undergoing a short course of instruction periodically, as is the case with officers and men of the mounted services.

Anyone who intends to ride a young horse, or to follow hounds for the first time in a season, should make sure that his grip is of sufficient strength. This is a point to which but little attention is paid, but it is of the greatest moment. Men who are constantly riding and who are in robust health, need not trouble themselves much about it. They know that, when necessary, they can take a good firm grip with their knees, but there are many who have no such certainty. The grip of the knees is required when jumping, or when the horse makes a sudden movement; it should not be constantly applied, for then the muscles would soon become useless from fatigue, but the rider should always be ready to apply it on the slightest warning. The power to grip can only be acquired by practice, and until that power is possessed there should be the greatest caution as to where one rides, and as to the kind of animal ridden. It may be incidently mentioned that an apparatus called "Savigear's Riding Grip Test," indicates the amount of pressure, in pounds, that a horseman can exert on the saddle with his knees, and that to ride safely he should be able to grip from seventy to a hundred pounds.

The following quotations from "The Book of Aids," are made *verbatim* in order that they may be thoroughly relied on by military riders. The comments deemed necessary for the purposes of this Guide are inserted in brackets.

MILITARY EQUITATION.

Military Equitation consists in the skilful and ready application of the Aids, by which the rider guides and controls the Horse in all his paces; and in a settled balance of the body, which enables him to preserve a firm seat in every variety of movement.

The Aids in Horsemanship are—the motions and proper application of the bridle hand and legs, to direct and determine the turnings and paces of the Horse.

This Science is indispensably requisite for the Military Horseman, in order that, being able to govern his horse by the aid of his legs and bridle hand, he may have the right hand at full liberty for the use of his weapons, and be capable on all occasions, whether acting singly or in a squadron, of performing with ease his various duties.

The system of Equitation laid down in the following pages is calculated to ensure these advantages—the rider, by the constant attention which is called forth in the practice of these lessons, will acquire intelligence and confidence; and the horse, being accustomed to yield to the impulse he receives from the rider, will be rendered supple, active and obedient.

SADDLING.

The saddle should be placed in the middle of the horse's back; the front of it about the breadth of the hand behind the play of the shoulder.

The numnah should be raised well into the fork over the withers by putting the arm under it.

The girth should admit a finger between it and the horse's belly. In saddling a horse, the girth must be tightened gradually, and not with violence. It is recommended that the girths of all except young and growing horses should be fitted so as to be worn at home in the second or third hole from the free end of the girth strap.

The surcingle should lie flat over, and not tighter than the girth.

The breastplate should be so fitted that the upper edge of the rosette or leather is the breadth of three fingers above the sharp breast-bone. It should admit the breadth of the hand between it and the flat of the shoulder, and also between the martingale (when used) and the horse's chest.

The carbine-bucket should hang perpendicularly; the butt-plate of the carbine should be as nearly as possible the breadth of four fingers below the elbow.

The blanket is folded lengthways in three equal folds, one end is then turned over 24 inches, the other is turned into the pocket formed by the folds, the blanket, thus folded, is placed on the horse's back with the thick part near the withers. Size when folded 2' 2" × 1' 8", when unfolded 5' 5" × 4' 8". The folding of the blanket may be modified to suit horses of peculiar conformation.

BRIDLING.

The bridoon should touch the corners of the mouth, but should hang low enough not to wrinkle them.

The bit should be placed in the mouth so that the mouthpiece is one inch above the lower tusk of a horse, and two inches above the corner tooth of a mare. This can only be laid down as a general rule, however, as so much depends on the shape and sensitiveness of the horse's mouth, and on his temper.

The curb should be laid flat and smooth under the jaw, and should admit two fingers easily between it and the jawbone.

The headstall should be parallel to and behind the cheekbone

The noseband should be the breadth of two fingers below the cheekbone, and should admit two fingers between it and the nose.

The throat lash should admit two fingers between it and the horse's jaw.

The bridoon rein should be of such a length that, when held by the middle, in the full of the left hand, with a light feeling of the horse's mouth, it will touch the rider's waist.

Leading and standing to the horse.

The man standing on the near side of the horse, the bridoon reins are to be taken over the head, held with the right hand, the forefinger between them, near the rings of the bridoon; the right arm bent, the hand as high as the shoulder; the end of the reins in the left hand, which hangs down without constraint behind the thigh.

When leading through a doorway, the man, still holding the end of the bridoon reins in the left hand, places himself in front of his horse, and taking one rein in each hand, close to the rings of the bridoon, steps backwards, taking care that the horse's hips clear the posts of the door. When the horse is through he places himself on the near side, as before.

In passing an officer the soldier should look towards him without changing his position, and filing past an officer for inspection the man should lead on the same flank as that on which the officer is standing.

"In Front of your Horses."

Each man will take a full pace forward with the right foot, turning to the right-about on the ball of it, and take the bridoon reins in each hand near the rings, still holding the end of them in the left hand, raising the horse's head to the height of his own breast and six inches from it, and making the horse stand even; hands and elbows as high as the shoulders. (In this position a man shows a horse to an officer when halted.)

"Eyes Right (or left) Dress."

When fronting the horses, the men will dress to the same flank as when mounted.

"Off side, stand to your Horses."

Each man will take a full pace forward with the left foot to the horse's off side, turning right about on the ball of it, and coming to "Attention," the left hand holding the reins near the rings, the forefinger between them, and the right hand taking hold of the end of the reins and hanging down behind the thigh.

"In Front of your Horses."

Each man will take a full pace forward with the left foot, turn left about on it, and resume the position before described, the left hand taking the end of the reins.

"Stand to your Horses."

Each man will take a full step forward with the right foot to the horse's near side, and turn left-about on the ball of it, coming to "Attention."

"In Front of your Horses."

As before described.

"Single file right," "Quick March."

Each man will turn to his left and move off in succession, dropping his left hand, which holds the ends of the reins, to the side, and holding the reins with the right hand as before directed, a horse's length distance being preserved from nose to croup.

(For "Single file left" the instruction is similar, the words "right" and "left" being substituted for each other.)

The recruits will next be instructed in the preceding positions and movements when the reins are put over the horses' heads and hanging on their necks.

"Stand at Ease."

Each man will draw back the right foot, as in foot drill, but the right hand will slide down the bridoon rein to the full extent of the arm, the rein being retained in the hand, and the left hand will hang down behind the thigh.

"Attention."

As before directed, but holding the left rein near the ring, the right hand raised as high as the man's shoulder, the left hand hanging down straight by the thigh.

"In Front of your Horses, &c."

As before directed, except that in all cases only one rein is held in each hand.

[It is held to be, as a rule, better for beginners that their first lessons should be given on saddles with stirrups. By this means they gain confidence, and the muscles of their legs become stronger. They are also able to assume a more correct position on horseback. But after eight or ten lessons of this kind, most of them may be fit to ride without stirrups. It has almost invariably been observed that when young men commence on a numnah they cling by the lower part of the leg, or by the heel, while if riding on a saddle without stirrups, they take the additional precaution of holding on by the saddle, or by a friendly wallet, when their instructor is not supposed to be looking. The consequence is that bad habits are formed, which cannot easily be given up. This is especially noticeable with regard to the use of the lower part of the leg in holding on, which is a habit acquired in riding without stirrups before being prepared for it. The rider will, therefore, at this stage be taught to mount and dismount with stirrups, and will be placed in the proper position with stirrups (see page 53). When pupils have become tolerably confirmed in that position, and when they show some confidence, and strength of seat, they should be required to ride without stirrups. The latter exercise is absolutely necessary if an independent seat is to be acquired. Riding without stirrups, if persevered in, secures the rider's balance, and so does away with the need, that many riders feel, of hanging on by the bridle].

RIDING WITHOUT SADDLES.

Mounting and Dismounting with Numnahs.

The recruits will then be practised in mounting and dismounting. The reins having been put over the horse's head, and hanging evenly on his neck, the word will be given.

" Prepare to Mount."

On this caution, each man will turn to the right, step six inches to the right, and close the left heel.

He will hold the reins equally divided in the full of the left hand, which will be placed on the horse's withers. The right arm will be laid on the horse's loins, the forearm being well to the off side, and the fingers of the right hand closed.

"Mount."

By bending both knees, making a spring from the insteps, and assisting himself by straightening his arms, the man will raise himself as much as possible over his horse, and then pass his right leg over the horse and drop into his seat in the centre of the horse's back. In doing this he must be careful not to cling to the numnah, which would otherwise become displaced. He may hold the horse's withers with his left hand, but the fingers of the right hand must be kept closed, and the right arm only used by pressing the forearm against the off side of the horse.

"Prepare to Dismount."

On this caution, each man will place both his hands on his horse's withers, and raise himself from the horse's back by straightening his arms.

"Dismount."

He will bring his right leg clear over his horse's quarters and alight on the ground, throwing his weight on his toes. He will then step six inches to his left, close his right heel and turn to the left, laying hold of the bridoon rein.

Mounting and dismounting should also be practised on the off side.

As soon as the recruits are perfect in the detailed motions of mounting and dismounting, they must be practised in mounting and dismounting without pausing between the several motions.

Position with Numnahs.

The recruits being mounted will now be placed in the proper mounted position.

Each man should have his body balanced in the middle of the horse's back, head erect and square to the front, shoulders well thrown back, chest advanced, small of the back slightly bent forward, upper part of the arms hanging straight down from the shoulder, elbows bent and lightly closed to the hips, little fingers on a level with the elbows, wrists rounded, knuckles to the front, and thumbs pointing across the body. Each hand should hold a rein between the third and fourth finger, the end being thrown over the forefinger and the thumb closed upon it; when the horse is in motion the hands should be about three inches from the body, and from four to six inches apart, but when sitting at ease they should be close together and rest on the horse's withers, right hand over the left. The thigh should be stretched down from the hip, the flat of the thigh close to the horse's side, the knees a little bent, and the legs hanging down from the knee and near the horse's sides. The heels should be well stretched down, and the toes raised from the insteps, and as near the horse's sides as the heels. A plummet line from the front point of the shoulder should fall one inch behind the heels.

While following these instructions, the man must, however, sit easily on his horse, without having his muscles unnaturally braced, and without stiffness. In order to get his toes and heels into a proper position, he should be taught to turn the flat part of the thigh from the hip towards the horse's side, and not merely to twist the foot inwards from the ankle or knee.

This is the position halted, or at the walk; at the trot the body must be inclined a little backward, the whole figure pliant, and accompaning the movements of the horse. The elbows and lower limbs must be kept steady.

DRESSING AT THE HALT.

The recruits will next be instructed in taking up the proper dressing when mounted.

"Eyes Right (or Left) Dress."

The whole of the squad will take up the dressing by the flank named. The flank man and the man next to him will place themselves with their horses square across the school with one horse's length interval between them, and with their hind feet three yards from the side of the school. The remainder aligning themselves on them and keeping the same interval from man to man.

Each man will have his body quite square to the front, his head well up and just turned enough to allow a glance of the eye towards the dressing point, so as to be able to see the surface of the face of the next man but one.

A correct position must be retained while dressing, whether halted or moving, and no attempt must be made to get the dressing by leaning forward or backward.

"Eyes Front."

Each man will turn his head and look straight to his front.

EXTENSION AND BALANCE MOTIONS AT THE HALT.

[The Extension and Balance motions are excellent, but should first be done on foot. All pupils are recommended to get themselves into a state of modified athletic training before commencing a course of riding. If they do so, they will learn more quickly, and suffer less from muscular strain. The regulation physical drill, or simple dumb-bells, will help towards this end. The prescribed motions on horseback are beneficial to all horsemen, whatever may be their particular style of riding.]

In order to give the recruits ease and confidence while sitting on horseback, to teach them to preserve their balance under all circumstances, they will then be practised in the following extension and balance motions :—

"Prepare for Extension and Balance Motions."

On this caution each man will drop his reins on his horse's neck, and let his arms fall behind his thighs, hanging easily from his shoulders, with the palms of the hands to the front.

Caution,—" First Practice."

" One."

On the word " One," bring the hands, at the full extent of the arms, to the front, close to the body, knuckles downwards, till the fingers meet at the points; then raise them in a circular direction over the head, the ends of the fingers still touching and pointing downwards so as to touch the forage cap, thumbs pointing to the rear, elbows pressed back, shoulders kept down.

" Two."

On the word " Two," throw the hands up, extending the arms smartly upwards, palms of the hands inwards; then force them obliquely back, and gradually let them fall to the position of " Attention," elevating the neck and chest as much as possible.

"Three."

On the word " Three," raise the arms outwards from the sides without bending the elbow, pressing the shoulders back, until the hands meet above the head, palms to the front, fingers pointing upwards, thumbs locked, left thumb in front.

"Four."

On the word "Four," bend over until the hands touch the feet, keeping the arms and knees straight; after a slight pause, raise the body gradually, bring the arms to sides, and resume the position of "Attention."

N.B.—The foregoing motions are to be done slowly so that the muscles may be exerted throughout.

Caution,—"Second Practice."

"One."

On the word "One," raise the hands in front of the body, at the full extent of the arms, and in line with the mouth, palms meeting but without noise, thumbs close to the forefingers.

"Two."

On the word "Two," separate the hands smartly, throwing them well back, slanting downwards; at the same time raise the body on the fore part of the feet.

"One."......"Two,"

On the word "One," bring the arms forward to the position above described and so on.

"Three."

On the word "Three," smartly resume the position of "Attention."

In this practice, the second motion may be continued without repeating the words "One," "Two," by giving the order "Continue the Motions"; the squad will then take the time from the right hand man; on the word "Steady," the men will remain at the second position, and on the word "Three," they will resume the position of "Attention."

Caution,—"Third Practice."

The squad will make a second half turn to the right before commencing the third practice.

"One."

On the word "One," raise the hands with the fists clenched, in front of the body, at the full extent of the arms, and in line with the mouth, thumbs upwards, fingers touching.

"Two."

On the word "Two," separate the hands smartly, throwing the arms back in line with the shoulders, back of the hand downwards.

" Three.'

On the word " Three," swing the arms round as quickly as possible from front to rear.

" Steady."

On the word "Steady," resume the second position.

" Four."

On the word " Four," let the arms fall smartly to the position of " Attention."

Caution,—" Fourth Practice."
" One."

On the word " One," lean back until the head touches the horse's quarter, but moving the legs as little as possible.

" Two."

On the word " Two," resume the original position.

Caution,—" Fifth Practice."
" One."

On the word " One," lean down to the left side and touch the left foot with the left hand, without, however, drawing up the foot to meet the hand.

" Two."

On the word " Two," resume the original position.

The same practice should also be done to the right.

Caution,—"Sixth Practice."

"One."

On the word "One," pass the right leg over the horse's head, and turning in the seat, sit facing to the proper left, keeping the body upright and the hands resting on the knees.

"Two."

On the word "Two," pass the left leg over the horse's quarter, and, turning in the seat, sit facing to the rear, assuming as much as possible the proper mounted position, the arms hanging behind the thighs.

"Three."

On the word "Three," pass the right leg over the horse's quarter, and turning in the seat, sit facing to the proper right, the body upright, and the hands resting on the knees

"Four."

On the word "Four," pass the left leg over the horse's head, and, turning in the seat, resume the proper mounted position.

Each of the above motions may be performed by command of the instructor without repeating the words, "One," "Two," &c.

SIMPLE AIDS FOR MOVING OFF AT THE WALK, HALTING, REINING BACK, AND TURNING.

"Walk, March."

Each man will relax the feeling of the bridoon in his horse's mouth, by turning the little fingers of both hands towards the head of the horse; and will press both legs to the horse's sides. When the horse is in motion the hands should resume their position. The rate of the walk is four miles an hour.

"Halt."

Each man will feel both reins steadily by bringing his little fingers towards his breast, turning the nails upwards, and close both his legs for a moment, to keep the horse up to the hand. The feeling of the reins should be relaxed as soon as the horse is halted.

"Rein Back, March."

Each man will feel both reins lightly, by turning the little fingers towards the breast, and will press both legs to the horse's sides to raise his forehand and keep his haunches under him; the rider must not have a dead pull on the horse's mouth, but should ease the reins after every step, and feel them again.

"Halt."

Each man will ease both reins and feel them again, closing both legs for a moment to keep the horse up to the hand; the hands to be eased as soon as halted.

"Walk, March."

As before directed.

"Right (or Left) Turn."

The turn is made by a double feeling of the inward rein, the outward retaining a steady feeling, and the horse being kept up to the hand by a pressure of both legs, the outward leg the stronger.

[It often happens in "Right (or Left) Turn" that the inward leg is put on more strongly than the outward, and a jerk is given to the inward rein. The haunches of the horse are thus thrown out, instead of his hind feet being allowed to follow in the track of the fore. These points should receive special attention.]

"Right (or Left) About."

The aids for the turn about are as follows:—A double feeling of the inward rein and a stronger pressure of the inward leg, supported by the outward leg and rein, the horse turning on his centre, fore and hind feet describing a circle.

Walking and Trotting in the School or Manége.

The squad being now formed in line down the middle of the school, with a horse's length interval between the files, the instructor will proceed to move the squad across the school by the command, "Walk, March."

Correct dressing is to be kept by keeping the pace with an occasional glance of the eye. No turning of the head is to be permitted.

While moving in file round the school, the squad will be numbered off from the front as follows :—

"From the Front, Number."

The leading file tells off "One," the next "Two," and so on; each man turning his head to the inward hand while doing so, and at once turning his head again to the front.

"Trot."

Each man will ease his reins and press both legs to the horse, according to the horse's temper; when the horse is at the trot he should feel both reins, to raise the horse's forehand and keep his haunches under him.

"Walk."

By a steady feeling of both reins, each man will bring his horse to a walk. Both legs must, however, be pressed to the horse's sides to prevent him from altogether halting.

"Halt."

As before directed.

EXTENSION AND BALANCE MOTIONS WHILE MOVING.

As soon as the recruits have learned the proper method of moving their horses off at the walk and trot, and of bringing them again to the halt, the instructor will cause them to go round the school at the walk and trot without using their reins, folding their arms in front or behind their backs, or letting them hang straight from the shoulder, the reins being dropped on the horse's withers, and to do the extension and balance motions while their horses are in motion.

In order that the squad may be led at a steady and even pace, the instructor will name the men who are to ride without their reins at any particular time, taking care that the leading file is always riding with his reins.

Thus, the order will be given, " Nos. 2, 3, 4, &c." (or any other named men) " Drop your reins," " Arms hanging down," " In front (or behind your backs) fold your arms."

These men will then ride round the the school, or perform such extension and balance motions as may be directed, and, when the instructor thinks fit, will receive the command, " Take your reins."

The leading file will afterwards be changed, and the process will be repeated until the whole squad has been exercised.

In performing some of the extension motions (such as those which involve extending the arms to the right and left) while the squad is in motion, it will be necessary to make the squad file down the centre to give the necessary space. The leading file will lead down the centre of the school, and it will be found that the horses of the remainder will in most instances follow without the guidance of the reins, if the recruits are mounted upon thoroughly broken horses.

If any horse should break away from the others, or get so close to the horse in front as to be in danger of touching him, his rider must take up his reins to restore him to his place, and again drop them.

The instruction of recruits as above laid down, to be practised on horses with numnahs and bridoons, can only be carried out when a riding school or enclosed manége is available. When this is not the case, the preparatory instruction will commence at the beginning of the following section. It is of the utmost importance, however, that, whenever practicable, the instruction in the foregoing sections shall be thoroughly carried out.

MOUNTING AND DISMOUNTING WITHOUT STIRRUPS.

" Reins over."

The bit reins are passed over and in front of the bridoon, the bridoon reins are then passed over the horse's head, and the end of them brought over the left bit rein.

The recruits will lead their horses into the school, and will be formed up for instruction.

"Reins over."

The end of the bridoon reins is passed over the left bit rein and brought up over the horse's head.

They will then be instructed in mounting and dismounting without stirrups.

"Without Stirrups—Prepare to Mount."

As with numnahs, but left hand will be placed on the front of the saddle, the right hand being on the back of the saddle.

"Mount."

As with numnahs.

"Without Stirrups—Prepare to Dismount."

Each man will place both his hands, holding the reins, on the front of the saddle, with the fingers extended.

"Dismount."

As with numnahs.

As soon as the recruits are perfect in the detailed motions of mounting and dismounting, they must be practised in mounting and dismounting without pausing between the several motions.

The recruits being mounted, and having been taught to cross the stirrups, will be taught to assume the proper mounted position in the saddle.

"Cross Stirrups."

Each man will pass the off stirrup over the horse's neck, and then pass the near one over the off.

SALUTE WHEN MOUNTED.

When a dragoon, riding on the bit or on all four reins (but without arms), passes an officer, he should ride at Attention, casting his eyes towards him. If riding on the bridoon only, he will also raise the outward hand until the little finger is in line with the thumb of the inward hand.

A lancer, if his lance is at the Sling or Trail when he passes an officer, should bring his lance to the Carry, casting his eyes towards him.

A dragoon with a carbine, if he passes an officer, should bring his carbine to the Carry, casting his eyes towards him.

A dragoon with a sword drawn, if he passes an officer, should bring his sword to the Carry, casting his eyes towards him.

Position of Bridle Hand with the Bit.

The upper arm hanging straight down from the shoulder, the left elbow lightly touching the hip; the lower arm square to the upper; the hand opposite the centre of the body and three inches from it, the back of the hand to the front, wrist rounded outwards, thumb pointing across the body, little finger on a level with the elbow; the top of the thumb firmly closed on the bit reins, which are divided by the little finger; the bridoon reins, when working with the bit, to be held in the full of the bridle hand and apart from the bit reins, hanging over the forefinger.

The bridle hand will, at the halt, always rest on the cape, cloak, or front of the saddle, and when sitting at ease the grasp of the fingers should be relaxed to allow more liberty to the horse's head.

The little finger of the bridle hand has four lines of action, viz. :—

Towards the breast, towards the right shoulder, towards the left shoulder, and towards the horse's head. These motions should be made from the wrist, the arm being kept perfectly steady.

Halting.

In Halting, the little finger is turned upwards, towards the breast, and resumes its position as soon as the horse has halted.

Reining Back.

In Reining Back, these motions are repeated alternately at every step.

Turning to the Right and Right-about.

In Turning to the Right and Right-about, the little finger is turned, and the hand a little raised, towards the right shoulder.

Right Shoulder in.

In Right Shoulder in, on turning from the boards, the little finger is turned towards the right shoulder; when in Shoulder in, the little finger should work partly upwards, towards the breast, and partly towards the left shoulder, to keep the horse's shoulders leading.

Right Pass.

In Right Pass, the little finger is turned towards the right shoulder; if the forehand is too much advanced, the little finger is turned towards the body to check it.

Half Passage.

In Half Passage, the little finger is not so much turned to the right shoulder.

Working to the Left.

In Working to the Left, the same movements are made towards the left shoulder.

Moving Forward.

In Moving Forward, the little finger is turned towards the horse's head, to ease the reins for a moment.

"Take up your Bridoon Reins."

On the command "Take up your Bridoon Reins," when riding on the bit, the left bridoon rein is drawn through the left hand and placed over the bit reins, the left thumb being closed firmly on the bit reins and left bridoon rein; the right bridoon rein is then held in the right hand, as when riding on the bridoon.

"Bit Reins."

On the command "Bit Reins," when riding on all four reins the right hand drops the right bridoon rein, takes hold of the left bridoon rein close to the left hand, and draws the rein through the left hand until the centre of the bridoon rein is in the full of the left hand; the left thumb then closes firmly on the bit reins, the bridoon rein being in front of the bit reins, over the forefinger, and the right hand assumes its proper position behind the thigh.

When it is necessary to ride on all four reins, with sword drawn or lance at the Carry, the left bridoon rein is drawn through the left hand as before, the right bridoon rein is then placed across the left hand the reverse way of the left bridoon rein, and the left thumb closes firmly on all four reins.

Bridoon reins are always to be taken up when marching at ease, going over jumps, or manœuvring over bad ground.

Rising in Stirrup.

Recruits are to be instructed in Rising in Stirrup, which habit, being conducive to the greater ease of both man and horse, is to be encouraged and practised whenever possible.

[This is done by raising the body from the knees, with the help of foot-pressure on the stirrups. The leg from the knee downward, should be kept steady and the rider should rise not more than three or four inches, less if possible. It is certain that men cannot be taught to ride without sitting close and bumping, nor can they ever rise well in stirrups until they have got their balance, and been shaken into a good seat, by riding for some months without stirrups. Nevertheless all should learn to rise. The following remarks were made to the Aldershot Military Society by the late General Keith Fraser, when Inspector General of Cavalry :—" I believe Nolan who fell at Balaclava, who was one of the best cavalry soldiers that ever lived, and knew all about horses, said bobbing up and down would take more out of a man in ten miles than rising in the stirrup would do in fifty. I should like all the men to be taught to rise in their stirrups." The latter sentence was received with applause at the time, and has now been authoritatively endorsed.]

MOUNTING AND DISMOUNTING WITH STIRRUPS.

[The seven motions by which the rider is here taught to place himself on the horse's back, although when the orders are read or repeated they seem tedious and minute, are nevertheless the best known means of mounting a saddled and bridled horse. It cannot be done more quickly. When once a man has accustomed himself to mount and dismount in the manner laid down, the detail is found to be perfectly natural and suitable. He is in no danger of neglecting anything essential or of putting himself in an awkward position. The time occupied in accurately learning these motions will be time well spent, if the rider preserve, through life, the excellent habit of mounting and dismounting in this manner. When a soldier, or any rider, carrying a whip mounts a horse, he should hold the whip in the left hand together with the reins and a lock of the mane. This obviates the embarrassment observed when a man passes his leg over the saddle, if he holds the whip in the right hand.]

How many motions are there in Mounting?

Four in preparing to mount, and three in mounting.

What are the Motions in preparing to Mount?

1st Motion.

The man turns to the right on the left heel, and places his right foot opposite the stirrup and parallel to the horse, heels about six inches apart; thus fronting the horse, he takes the bridoon reins in the centre with the left hand; he then takes the end of the bit reins with the fore-finger and thumb of the right hand, placing the little finger of the left hand between them; the left hand is then placed below the right on the neck of the horse, about twelve inches from the saddle. The bridoon rein when used singly is to be taken in the same manner as the bit rein.

2nd Motion.

The right hand draws the reins through the left, and shortens them, so that the left has a light and equal feeling of both reins on the horse's mouth; the right hand remains over the left.

3rd Motion.

The right hand throws the reins to the off side, takes a lock of the mane, brings it through the left, and twists it round the left thumb; the left hand closes firmly on the mane and reins. The right hand now quits the mane and takes hold of the left stirrup, the fingers behind, and the thumb in front.

4th Motion.

The left foot is raised and put into the stirrup as far as the ball of it; the right hand is placed on the back part of the saddle. The left knee is placed against the saddle on the surcingle; the left heel is to be drawn back, in order to avoid touching the horse's side with the toe.

What are the Motions in Mounting?

1st Motion.

By a spring of the right foot from the instep the man raises himself in the stirrup, bringing both heels together, knees firm against the saddle, and the heels drawn back a little; the body erect and partially supported by the right hand.

2nd Motion.

The right hand moves from the back to the front of the saddle, and supports the the body, while the right leg passes clear over the horse's quarters to the off side; the right knee closes on the saddle, and the body comes gently into it.

3rd Motion.

The left hand quits the mane, the right the saddle, and the bridle hand assumes its proper position, and the right hand drops behind the thigh, without constraint; he is then able to take the stirrup with the right foot without the help of hand or eye.

Placing the foot in the Stirrup.

When the feet are in the stirrups the heels should be well sunk, and the feet retained in the stirrups by an easy play of the ankle and instep, the stirrup to be kept under the ball of the foot.

Position with Stirrups.

The position with stirrups is nearly the same as without stirrups, the knee being a little more bent.

A plummet line falling from the point of the knee should drop directly on the ball of the foot. The foot should be kept in its place by the play of the ankle and instep, the stirrup being under the ball of the foot. The lower edge of the bar is, as a general rule, to be from two and a half to three and a half fingers breadth above the upper edge of the heel of the boot, when the man is sitting in the proper position. The instructor must remember, however, that though he should follow the general rules in fitting the stirrups, a great deal depends on whether the rider has a thin flat thigh, or the reverse. A man with a thick thigh requires slightly shorter stirrups, otherwise, when the horse is in motion and the muscles are brought into play, he will not have a proper hold of the stirrups. The rider should be slowly trotted round the school or manége, and if a man is then seen to be well down in the saddle, with his leg in the proper position with his heel down, and yet not to have a proper hold of his stirrups, the stirrups require shortening.

[A general rule for the length of the stirrup leather on a plain saddle, is that, including the stirrup-iron, it should be the same length as the arm, measured from under the arm to the tips of the fingers. The leg, from the hip bone to the knee, will then form an angle of about 45 degrees].

How many motions are there in Dismounting?

Three in preparing to dismount, and four in dismounting.

What are the Motions in preparing to Dismount?

1st Motion.

The right hand takes hold of the bit reins above the left; the right foot quits the stirrup.

2nd Motion.

The right hand holds the reins, the left slides forward on them, about twelve inches from the saddle, feeling the horse's mouth very lightly.

3rd Motion.

The right hand drops the reins to the off side, takes a lock of the mane, brings it through the left, and twists it round the left thumb, the fingers of the left hand closing on it ; the right hand is then placed on the front of the saddle, the body to be kept erect.

What are the motions in Dismounting?

1st Motion.

Supporting the body with the right hand and left foot, the right leg is brought gently (without touching the horse's hind-quarters) to the near side, heels close ; the right hand on the back of the saddle is to preserve the balance of the body, as in mounting.

2nd Motion.

The body is gently lowered until the right toe touches the ground.

3rd Motion.

Resting on the right foot, the left stirrup is quitted and the left foot is placed in a line with the horse's fore feet ; the hands remain as in the former motion.

4th Motion.

Both hands quit their hold ; the man turns to the left, and brings the body square to the front ; during the turn the right hand lays hold of the bridoon rein, near the ring, and raises the horse's head as high as the man's shoulder.

[All horse-soldiers should learn to mount and dismount at the walk and canter. Disaster may occur if men cannot mount on the move, as in the case of the late Prince Imperial of France.]

Stand easy.

Whenever the men are dismounted, with or without arms, and have been allowed to Stand Easy from the position of Stand at Ease, they will be recalled to the latter position by the command "Stand to your Horses."

QUESTIONS AND ANSWERS ON THE SYSTEM OF MILITARY EQUITATION.

What is meant by Aids in horsemanship ?

The motions and proper application of the bridle hand and legs, to direct and determine the turnings and paces of the horse.

What Aids are required in turning to the right or left?

A stronger feeling of the inward rein; the outward retaining a steady feeling, the horse kept up to the hand by a pressure of both legs, the outward leg the stronger. In crossing the school an interval of three and a half yards from knee to knee to be kept, and ride at the regulation pace.

What is the first thing to be done in reining back?

Close both legs to the horse's sides.

When should reining back commence?

When the rider is sensible of every bearing of his hand on the horse's mouth and the pressure of his legs on the horse's sides.

How would you then proceed?

To rein back straight the little fingers must be turned towards the breast, and both legs must press equally the sides of the horse to compel him to collect himself, and prevent him from bearing on the bridle, and dragging his fore feet on the ground; the rider should not have a dead pull on his horse's mouth, but ease the reins after every step, and then feel them again.

What is the rider to guard against in reining back?

Allowing the horse to hurry or run back out of hand, diverging from a straight line, or halting in an uncollected position; but should press him well up to the bridle, so that his legs are properly placed, or immediately underneath his body.

Of what use is reining back?

To bring the greater weight from the forehand on the haunches, collecting and making him light in hand.

How to lead a horse into the corners.

Feel the outward rein and apply the inward leg, preserving the bend at the same time.

What Aids are required in turning right or left about?

A stronger feeling of the inward rein, and a stronger pressure of the inward leg, supported by the outward leg and rein, the horse turning on his centre, fore and hind feet describing a circle; when about, the dressing is changed.

How many ways are there of turning about?

Three; on the forehand, centre, and haunches.

What Aids are required to make a horse trot?

Each man will ease his reins and press both legs to his horse, according to the horse's temper; when the horse is at the trot he should feel both reins; to raise the horse's forehand and keep his haunches under him. The rate of the riding school trot is nine miles an hour.

What Aids are required in circling?

A stronger feeling of the inward rein, retaining a steady feeling of the outward, the horse to be well supported with the outward leg; if circling to the right, dressing to the right; if to the left, the dressing to the left, the ride turning with the leading file from the boards; and with the rear file on the centre of the school, arriving again at the boards with the leading file. An interval of three yards and a half from knee to knee in advancing and retiring, and four feet from head to croup at the centre and side. In circling, every man will make his horse describe a circle, supporting him well with the inward rein and the outward leg; if the circles are well made, the ride will cover on the centre. Follow the rear file two paces down the centre, and look to him for leaving.

What aids are required to make a horse halt?

A steady feeling of both reins, and closing both legs for a moment, to keep the horse well up to the hand; the hands to be eased as soon as halted.

What aids are required in bending a horse?

A light and playful feeling of the inward rein, supporting the horse at the same time with the outward leg and rein; the bend to be made from the pole of the neck. Bending and unbending should be gradual.

What aids are required in working shoulder in?

The outward rein leads, the inward preserves the bend, the inward leg presses the horse to cross his legs, the outward leg keeps him up to the hand and prevents him from swerving.

How should a horse be bent in shoulder in?

When a horse is properly bent in shoulder in, the whole body, from head to tail, should be curved, the shoulders leading, the inward legs crossing over the outward, fore and hind feet moving on two lines parallel to the side of the manége, hind feet one yard from the side.

How should a horse be turned when working shoulder in?

On the forehand; the inward rein staying his forehand, and a pressure of the inward leg circling his croup round; the outward leg and rein supporting; when turned, the shoulders are led off by the outward rein.

What aids are required in the passage?

The inward rein bends and leads the horse. The outward balances and assists the power of the inward; the outward leg makes him cross his legs and the inward keeps him up to the hand.

How should a horse be turned in the passage?

On the haunches; the inward leg staying his hind quarters, and a double feeling of the inward rein to circle his forehand round, the outward leg preventing his haunches flying out.

What aids are required in the half passage?

The horse's forehand should be brought

in by a double feeling of the inward rein, the outward leg closed so as to bring his hind quarters in an oblique direction, shoulders leading. Each file in succession when he arrives at the point where the leading file began the half passage, applies the same Aids and dresses with his horse's head on the outward knee of the man in front of him. The horse must bend and look the way he is going; the inward rein bends and leads, the outward assists and balances the power of the inward; the pressure of the outward leg obliges the horse to place one foot before the other; the inward leg keeps him up to the hand.

What is the difference between the full and half passage?

In the full passage the horse crosses his legs, in the half passage he only half crosses his legs, placing one foot before the other.

What is the difference between the passage and shoulder in?

In the passage the horse bends and looks the way he is going, the outward legs are crossing over the inward, and the inward rein leads; in shoulder in, the horse does not look the way he is going, the inward legs are crossing over the outward, and the outward rein leads.

How to halt a horse on the passage.

Feeling both reins and closing the inward leg.

How to halt a horse in shoulder in.

Feeling both reins and closing the outward leg.

Of what use is the shoulder in and passage?

To make the horse supple in the neck and ribs, to give a free action to his shoulders, and to teach him to obey the pressure of the leg.

What Aids are required in turning about on the forehand?

Stay the forehand with the inward rein, circle the croup round with the outward leg, the outward rein well supporting, and the inward leg keeping him up to the hand.

What Aids are required in turning about on the haunches?

Stay the hind quarters with the inward leg, circle the forehand round with the inward rein, the outward leg and rein well supporting, to prevent the haunches flying out.

What is the object of turning about on the
  forehand?

To teach the horse to obey the pressure
of the leg.

What is the object of turning about on the
  haunches?

To teach the horse to follow the rein.

What is the object of turning about on the
  centre?

To teach the horse to obey the leg and
rein.

What Aids are required in coming from
  right shoulder in to right pass?

Closing the left leg, and leading the
shoulders off with the right rein.

What Aids are required in coming from
  right pass to left shoulder in?

Change the position of the horse's head,
stay the forehand with the left rein, and
circle the croup round with the left leg;
right leg and rein well supporting; when
turned the shoulders led off with the right
rein.

What Aids are required in coming from
  right shoulder in to right pass shoulder
  out?

A double feeling of the left rein, and a stronger pressure of the left leg; the horse turning on his centre; the right leg and rein well supporting; when turned, shoulders led off with the right rein.

What Aids are required in coming from right pass shoulder out to right shoulder in?

A double feeling of the right rein, and a stronger pressure of the right leg; the horse turning on his centre; left rein and leg well supporting; when turned, shoulders led off with the left rein.

What Aids are required in cantering?

A light and firm feeling of both reins to raise the horse's forehand; a pressure of both legs to bring his haunches under him; a double feeling of the inward rein, and a stronger pressure of the outward leg will oblige the horse to strike off true and united.

What does cantering false mean?

In cantering to the right, the horse leading with both near legs is false; if to the left, leading with both off legs.

What does cantering disunited mean?

Cantering with the off fore and near hind, or near fore and off hind.

Cantering true and united.

Cantering with the off fore followed by the off hind, if to the right; the near fore followed by near hind, if to the left.

How is the pressure of the legs to be applied?

The pressure of the legs must be an elastic feeling of the muscles—not a dull and heavy clinging or kicking of the limbs.

[The pressure must not be applied with the back part of the calf of the leg. The knees must be kept close to the saddle, and the feet remain parallel to the horse, while the leg is drawn back slightly, and pressed against the horse just behind the girths.]

What does fineness of mouth mean?

Fineness of mouth means a mouth that is perfectly trained, and that responds to the action of the bridle hand; therefore the rider cannot be too cautious in the manner in which he uses the bit reins, or too careful that the movements of his hand are the correct indications of his own will; always bearing in mind that fineness of mouth is not produced by lacerating the gums of the horse, as the delicate skin which covers them is never so tender and sensitive after abrasion as before.

Are all horses alike delicate in the feeling upon the bars of the mouth?

They are, except when, from the use of severe bits and a heavy hand, the sensibility of touch has been destroyed.

Is the yielding and lightness of the horse caused by the delicacy of his mouth?

It is not.

How is it then caused?

By the suppleness of the neck and shoulders combined with that of the ribs and haunches, and also the perfect balance of the horse.

What is meant by a horse being balanced?

When a horse has become so far suppled, and obedient to the Aids, as to have his powers fairly concentrated between the hand and leg of the rider.

In applying the Aids, do the hand and leg work together?

Yes. The simultaneous application of hand and leg is the essential groundwork of good horsemanship. It is begun and continued throughout every pace of the horse, and without it there never will be good riding on the part of the rider, nor collected action on the part of the horse.

What has the rider to guard against in applying the Aids?

The rider must be ever cautious when he makes any increased bearing or pressure with one hand or leg, that he does not cease to have a proper feeling upon the horse with the other hand and leg also; otherwise the bridle will have an imperfect bearing upon the horse's mouth, and want of due pressure with the legs will tend to render the horse uncollected in his action.*

What is meant by a horse being behind the hand?

A horse may be said to be behind the hand when, in reining back, he evades the feeling of the bit, and closing of the legs, by lowering his forehand, and not facing his bridle, or by breaking his paces when upon the move.

How is this generally caused?

It may proceed from several causes, such as the rider not supporting the horse sufficiently with the leg, thereby throwing the weight too much upon the forehand, or by

---

* Particular attention is directed to the above Aid.

a hard unyielding hand, or by weakness and want of power in applying the Aids; or, lastly, by want of strength or steadiness in the seat.

Are all horses capable of being suppled and rendered obedient to the Aids?

They are; but it is a work of far greater difficulty to supple old horses than young ones; it requires also much care, patience, and skill to supple those of naturally bad formation.

When horses are not obedient to the riders should resource be had to punishment?

If the proper method be used, it very rarely happens that there is any want of obedience on the part of the horse; punishment is therefore unnecessary, and as a rule should not be allowed, except by the most experienced men, and then only, as a last resource.

In the case of resistance what are the means to be resorted to?

Resistance being frequently caused by the rider exacting more from the horse than his suppleness and formation enable him to perform, the most simple lessons should be resorted to, and patiently continued until the horse becomes more supple, and consequently obedient.

Is it to be considered that men or horses, after being brought to a state of perfection in training, will continue so without the practice being kept up?

The fact of men or horses having been once brought to a state of perfection in training must by no means be considered sufficient, as the men cannot get experience except by repeated lessons, and the horses will lose much of their suppleness if not kept up to it. Too much attention therefore, cannot be given to the continued practice in Military Equitation of the trained men and horses.

Should the action or motion of the horse (at any pace) at all interfere with the fairness or steadiness of the rider's hand?

Certainly not; the rider who cannot control the motions of his hand must be said to have "no hand"; it therefore requires an independent seat to have a "good hand."

Standing leap.

Bring the horse up to the bar at an animated walk, halt him with a light hand upon the haunches; when rising, only feel the reins so as to prevent them becoming slack; when the horse springs forward, yield them without reserve; when the horse's hind feet come to the ground, again collect him moving on at the same pace; checking the horse after he has made the leap must be particularly avoided, as he takes it as a punishment, when he ought to be encouraged, and becomes shy of the leap next time.

Open ditch.

The horse should be brought up to an animated pace, and kept steady and straight to the jump; the rider must depend upon the judgment of the horse for the distance he will take to make the spring, taking care to keep his body back, and legs close to the horse's side, bridle hand firm, and the spur ready to be applied if necessary at the moment of the spring.

[The body need not be leaned back in any great degree, at an open ditch or long leap, but the above instruction may be useful in counteracting the natural tendency of a young rider to lean forward. In point of fact, the preferable position is upright, leaning neither back nor forward.

Keep the horse's head straight for the leap, with reins in each hand. The knees holding tight, and the legs on, behind the girths. Reserve the tight closing of the knees until you are within a few yards of the jump, give him his head when he rises, lean back when he is coming down, pick him up when he has landed, and then move on at the original pace. Take care not to pull him up too soon or he may land in the middle of the jump. Buck jumps, three feet high and ten feet apart, afford excelent practice, when once a strong seat has been secured; tilting at the ring, picking up a stirrup-iron with a lance pole, and other exercises, may be practised when riders are well advanced.]

Flying leap.

The horse must not be hurried, or allowed to rush, but with a light and steady hand keep his head steady and straight to the bar; position the same as in the standing leap.

Swimming a horse.

Occasion may occur on service when a dragoon may be obliged to swim his horse. If he knows how to do so, it may be done with safety. Ignorance of the proper mode may be fatal to both man and horse. The rider should take up and cross his stirrups to prevent the horse entangling himself with them; he should quit the bit rein, and scarcely feel the bridoon, and any attempt to guide the horse must be by the slightest touch possible; he should lean his chest as much over the horse's withers as he can, throwing his weight forward, and holding the mane to prevent the rush of water carrying him backwards. If the horse appears distressed, a man who cannot swim may with safety hold the mane and throw himself out flat on the water, thereby relieving the horse from his weight; when the horse comes into his depth he may again drop into the saddle.

What Aids are required to incline?

A double feeling of the inward rein, supported by a pressure of the outward leg.

How should the dressing be taken?

The leading file keeps the direction, the remainder conform to him, and dress by seeing the cheek and back of the shoulder of the second file from him, keeping three yards and a half from knee to knee.

CROSS AIDS.

Aids from right half pass to left shoulder in.

Change the position of the horse's head, stay the forehand with the left rein, circle the croup round with the left leg, then lead the shoulders off with the right rein.

Aids from right half pass to left half pass.

Change the position of the horse's head, close the right leg, and lead the shoulders off with the left rein.

Aids from right half pass to right pass shoulder in.

Stay the forehand with the right rein, circle the croup round with the left leg, when turned lead the shoulders off with the right rein.

Aids from right half pass to left pass shoulder out.

Change the position of the horse's head, stay the forehand with the left rein, circle the croup round with the right leg, when turned lead the shoulders off with the left rein.

Aids from right pass to right pass shoulder out.

Stay the hind quarters with the right leg, circle the forehand round with the right rein, the left leg closed to prevent the haunches flying out.

Aids from right pass shoulder out to left pass shoulder in.

A double feeling of the right rein, a stronger pressure of the right leg supported by the left leg and rein, the horse turning on his centre; when turned, change the position of the horse's head, and lead the shoulders off with the left rein.

Aids from right pass shoulder in to left pass shoulder out.

The same as the preceding answer.

Aids from right pass shoulder in to left shoulder in.

Change the position of the horse's head, and lead the shoulders off with the right rein.

Aids from right pass to right pass shoulder in.

Stay the forehand with the right rein, circle the croup round with the left leg; when turned, lead the shoulders off with the right rein.

Aids from right pass to left pass shoulder out.

Change the position of the horse's head, stay the forehand with the left rein, circle the croup round with the right leg; when turned, lead the shoulders off with the left rein.

Note.—To question these Aids as performed from the left rein, it will only be necessary to substitute in the questions and answers " Left " for " Right " and " Right " for " Left."

RIDING WITH THE SWORD.

When standing to his horse at " Attention," the dragoon with a sword stands square to the front with his toes in line with his horse's fore feet, holding the bridoon rein with the right hand near the bit, the right hand raised as high as his own shoulder, the sword upright by the side as on foot parade.

" Stand at Ease."

The position of the man is the same as in the foot drill, except that the right hand slides down the bridoon rein to the full extent of the arm, the rein being retained in the hand.

" By numbers." " Prepare to Mount," [In four motions.]
As before directed.

" Mount." [In three motions.]
As before directed.

" Prepare to Dismount." [In three motions.]
As before directed.

" Dismount." [In four motions.]
As before directed.

In mounting on the off side, the dragoon will pass the sword over behind him, as he is bringing down his left leg into the saddle. In dismounting on the off side, the sword is first to be laid across the front of the saddle, the shoe of the scabbard to the right.

" Draw Swords."

(1) Pass the right hand smartly across the body, over the bridle arm, to the sword knot,* place it on the wrist, give it two turns inwards to secure it, and as the handle is grasped draw out the blade

---

* When the sword is attached to the saddle, it may be necessary to draw out the blade so as to rest the hilt on the bridle arm before the sword knot is taken and the handle properly grasped.

slowly† until the hand is in line with the elbow, turning the edge to the rear, the right arm close to the body, shoulders square to the front. (2) With an extended arm draw the sword slowly from the scabbard, edge to the rear, in rear of left shoulder, and bring it smartly to the "Recover," that is, with the bar of the hilt in line with the bottom of the chin, blade perpendicular, edge to the left, elbow close to the body. (3) Lower the sword smartly to the "Carry," that is, with the hilt resting on the thigh, blade perpendicular, edge slightly inclined to the left, the grasp of the lower fingers slightly relaxed, little finger in rear of the hilt, arm close to the body, that part of it between the wrist and the elbow lightly touching the hip.

"Slope Swords."

Bring the lower part of the arm at right angles to the upper, hand in front of the elbow, relax the grasp of the second and third fingers, and allow the sword to fall lightly on the shoulder, midway between the neck and point of the shoulder, the little finger still in rear of the hilt.

---

† Swords must be drawn from and returned to the scabbards SLOWLY, in order to preserve the edge.

"Sit at Ease."

Keeping the sword at the slope, place the hands on the front part of the saddle, with the right hand over the left.

"Attention."

Come smartly to the position of "Slope Swords."

"Carry Swords."

Resume the grasp of the second and third fingers and bring the blade perpendicular, the hilt resting on the thigh, as in the third motion of drawing swords,

"Return Swords."

Carry the hilt smartly to the hollow of the left shoulder, blade perpendicular, edge to the left, elbow level with shoulder; then, by a quick turn of the wrist, drop the point in rear of left shoulder slowly into the scabbard, and resume the position at the end of the first motion of "Draw Swords," shoulders being kept square to the front throughout this motion. (2) Return the sword slowly into the scabbard, release the hand from the sword knot by giving it two turns outwards, the right hand remaining across the body in line with the elbow, fingers extended and close together, back of the hand up. (3) Drop the right hand smartly to the side.

When " Draw Swords" is ordered at the walk, the men, after drawing, will remain at the " Carry " until ordered to " Slope "; but if " Draw Swords " is ordered at the trot or gallop, the men will come to the " Slope " after drawing.

When men are dismounted to lead their horses, or attack on foot with carbines, swords are to be attached to the saddles.

Proving.

In proving the telling off with a drawn sword, the sword is brought to the "Carry," and again sloped on the command " *As you were.*"

[The ride should be frequently halted for the purpose of correcting the position of the riders and giving them the hints which they may individually require. No one under instruction should be allowed to carry a whip in the school without leave, and all should be taught to treat the horses in the kindest and most friendly manner. They should especially be made to understand the delicate structure of the horse's mouth. A Riding Master should be quiet and patient but firm, and should not attempt to push his pupils too rapidly on. He should be able to gauge the ability of each man, never expecting more from him than the instruction he has received should enable him to perform. If requisite, he should, again and again, explain lucidly and without loss of temper, such points as may not have been comprehended by members of the ride, and he should give the reasons for the various applications of the aids, so that all may work intelligently together. It is almost unnecessary to add that an absolutely correct standard of conduct and language should be scrupulously maintained in every riding school. Assistants should not be allowed to carry whips, and interfere with the pace of the ride. That should be kept exclusively in the hand of the Master.]

LADIES' EQUITATION.

Let us glance for a moment at the lady, the horse, the saddle, and the habit, each and all of which must receive careful attention, before the combined effect can be pronounced satisfactory. Although riding is pre-eminently the exercise which gives beauty and grace to the female face and form, yet it is well to prepare for a course of instruction by a few simple exercises on foot. The more arduous exertions in the saddle will be all the easier, and the lessons will be all the sooner learned, if the muscles be strong and the frame supple and erect. In these days when cycling and tennis are universally in favour, it should perhaps be taken for granted that all young ladies are quite fit to begin riding, with pleasure and profit to themselves; but if any of them desire a series of exercises requiring no apparatus, the first five Extension and

Balance Motions (p. 31) may be recommended. These can be performed on foot just as well as on horseback, substituting for the fourth practice the following :—Bend slowly backward and then forward, as far as possible, without bending the knees; and substituting for the fifth practice the following :—Lean to the right and left alternately, touching the leg as near the foot as possible.

THE LADY'S HORSE.

The lady's horse should be perfectly broken as well as naturally docile, with a good mouth and safe action. A proper average height for a lady's horse is 15 hands. Much depends on the taste of the rider, but, as a rule, anything above 15.2 is too conspicuous. It is, of course, desirable that he should be handsome and well bred, but it must likewise be remembered that a tall and well grown horsewoman always looks best when mounted on a horse of some substance, provided that he has good action, a fine coat, and tolerably good looks. A smaller lady should ride a smaller animal, but each should ride the horse that suits her best in its size, style and paces.

THE SIDE SADDLE.

With regard to the side saddle, some caution should be exercised. It is not always practicable to keep a saddle for each horse, although it would be very desirable to do so, but the next best thing is to get a saddle that fits the lady. It can then be stuffed as required, for any horse that has to carry it. These saddles vary in length from 16 to 21 inches; and of course they vary in age and weight. The best plan is to try a number of old saddles until a really good and comfortable fit is found, when one of the same dimensions may be ordered from an expert in the making of ladies' saddles. Second-hand saddles are frequently unsatisfactory. The same sidesaddle has been known to change hands several times in one year, having been in each case sold for much less than was paid for it. To order a new saddle that will fit the rider is probably the best economy. With very young riders it has, doubtless, a good effect to let them ride both on the near and off side, but when they are grown up it is better to let the habit of riding on one side become second nature and not disturb it.

THE RIDING HABIT.

The skirt should be fitted when the wearer is on horseback. The whole habit should be quiet in colour, neat and severely simple in style, avoiding extremes in length or shortness, and should fit with perfect ease and comfort. A good habit maker will be able to give ladies information as to other items of a horsewoman's outfit. Suffice it to say that hat, gloves and whip should be suitable to the wearer; the hair should be done up tightly, no ear-rings should be worn, and the whip should be of moderate length and almost inflexible. A safety skirt is not a necessity, but it may be recommended, as being safer than the ordinary one in case of a fall.

LADIES TO UNDERSTAND SADDLING AND BRIDLING.

Ladies should be carefully and repeatedly instructed in the various items which come under the head of Bridling in the foregoing pages, and also in those included under Saddling, so far as they apply to a lady's saddle (see p. 19), they will find the knowledge and experience thus obtained most useful in enabling them, when a horse is brought round, to see at a glance whether he is turned out comfortably and correctly. Restiveness and accidents may thus be obviated, for when a horse becomes unmanageable it is generally from preventable causes.

LADIES MOUNTING AND DISMOUNTING.

To mount her horse, a lady walks up close to the saddle, takes the snaffle reins with the left hand and places them with the whip in the right hand, with which she then takes hold of the top crutch. The lady next turns to the left, facing in the same direction as the horse, places her left hand on the left shoulder of the mounting assistant, and her left foot in the palms of his hands. Then, on the word *mount*, she straightens the left knee, springing from the right foot, while the assistant, who must be close to the horse, raises himself erect, and the lady is placed on the saddle. She faces to the left, and with the right hand on the crutch and the other on the cantle, slightly raises herself, and the assistant pulls her skirt straight and smooth. The lady next carries the right leg over the top of the crutch, rests it on the pommel, and places the ball of her left foot on the stirrup-iron, changing the reins to the left hand.

To dismount, take the reins in the right hand, bring the right leg over the crutch, and take the left foot out of the stirrup; see that the skirt is all clear, take hold of both crutches, and lower the body lightly to the ground. Or, dismount with the left hand on a man's arm and the right on the top crutch.

To mount without help, face the saddle, put the reins on the left arm, let out the stirrup leather, take hold of the lower crutch with the left hand, in which also hold the whip, then take the stirrup in the right hand and the reins in the left, put the right foot in the stirrup, taking care that the toe does not touch the horse's side, place the right hand on the top crutch, and spring into the saddle from the left foot, while pulling with both hands. Then settle the seat as usual, and correct the length of the stirrup.

THE LADY'S POSITION IN THE SADDLE.

The lady should sit quite square to the front, and she will be the better able to do so if, when settling down in her seat, she throws her right shoulder well back and looks, for a moment, to her right rear. This will bring her into a straightforward position in the centre of the saddle, which she should endeavour to maintain, keeping body and head erect.

The shoulders should be thrown well back, and be kept level. There should be the breadth of a finger between the calf of the right leg and the crutch, the right heel should be a little drawn back, and the toes of each foot should point to the front. The stirrup will be the right length if the rider can insert the palm of her left hand between her leg and the crutch when the knee is bent. If the stirrup leather is shorter, the knee is likely to be bruised, and if longer there will be an extra bearing on the off side, which means a bad seat, and a probable sore shoulder for the horse. The weight of the rider should be in the middle of the saddle, and by no means on the back part of it. This is a most necessary warning, because the backs of ladies' horses are more frequently injured by the weight which their riders place far back in the saddle, than by any other cause. It is an open question, whether side-saddles should not be so made that the rider cannot put her weight too far back, but it is, at least right, to point out that prevalent error, which each horsewoman should try to rectify for herself.

THE LADY'S REINS.

The little finger of the bridle hand should be placed between the reins when a single rein bridle is used, and after a light and even feeling of the mouth has been obtained, the end should be passed over the forefinger, and the thumb should be closed on the reins. When a double rein bridle is used, the third finger of the bridle hand is placed between the curb reins, and the last three fingers between the snaffle reins, the ends of both being turned over the fore finger, and the thumb closed on them, thus the little finger divides the near, and the second finger the off reins. This is preferable to holding the reins in the reverse position, viz.: with the third finger between the snaffle reins, and the curb reins outside; the greater leverage should, of course, be on the snaffle. When a lady rides with the reins in both hands, if a single rein bridle is used, she passes the near rein between the third and little fingers of the left hand, and the off rein between the corresponding fingers of the right hand. The free part of the rein, if any, should be passed over the left forefinger with the thumb pressed on it. When both hands are employed with a double rein bridle, the little finger of the right hand is placed between the off reins, the snaffle rein being outside. As a rule there should be a stronger feeling on the snaffle than on the curb reins, but they should all convey the gentle and yielding pressure which comes from lightness of hand. The thumb of the bridle hand should point across the body, the wrist be rounded outwards, and be held about four inches from the body, and not higher than the elbow. When reins are in both hands, the distance between the hands should be from four to six inches. The elbows should be close to the sides, and the arms perpendicular from the shoulder to the elbow.

It is however, not to be expected that any lady can manage her bridle hand with dexterity, or with comfort to herself and her horse, until she has learned by assiduous practice, to sit firmly and easily in her saddle; she may then change her reins from one hand to the other, drop them on the horse's withers, and take them up with the right hand or the left, disposing of them in the way already described. Facility in handling the reins, and in placing them with precision and fineness of touch, between the proper fingers, is of the utmost importance to the horsewoman, and is an accomplishment that will go far to insure her safety on horseback. By perseverance it will become as easy as knitting, or any other movement of the hands, that is mechanically performed.

When a lady has learned to mount, and been placed in the correct position on horseback, she should be directed to ride round the school or manége at a walk, and until her seat has been fairly confirmed she should have a snaffle bridle only, and hold a rein in each hand. The exercises for ladies should begin at "Walk, March," (p. 39), and should be carried on in accordance with the quotations from "The Book of Aids," so far as they are applicable to ladies. To obviate repetition, ladies and instructors are referred to that portion of the Guide.

In all the exercises in which the pressure of both legs is prescribed, it is to be understood, that the pressure of the lady's whip answers to that of the right leg. When a lady moves from the halt to the walk she brings back the left heel and touches the horse with her whip on the off side, at the same time easing the reins. When the horse moves she feels the reins again. The same aids are applied for the trot: but for the canter the whip should be applied on the off shoulder when cantering to the right, and on the near shoulder when cantering to the left. It is easier for a lady on an ordinary side saddle when her horse canters to the right or, in other words, leads off with the right foot. The most difficult pace is the trot. In order to be able to trot well and have a thoroughly independent seat, a lady should ride under instruction for three months without rising. At the end of that time she will probably be beautifully balanced, feel absolutely safe, have a firm seat and perfect hands, and be able to go anywhere. It may be said that the ordeal is severe, but on the other hand the results are most gratifying. The rise at the trot can then be done with evident ease and with only a slight motion. The rider is square to her front and sits in the centre of her saddle. If those ladies who ride obliquely, facing their left front, swinging their legs and rising high in the air, could see themselves at the trot as others see them, they would be ready to suffer much inconvenience and make great sacrifices to unlearn so unsightly and injurious a habit It must not, however, be inferred that to become a fairly good rider a lady requires three months without rising in the stirrup. A shorter time may make a considerable improvement, but as with soldiers, so with horsewomen, it is the long period without rising that gives the strongest and best seat and consequently the best hands.

With regard to the general principle, some writers insist that until beginners have been well established in the saddle they should not be allowed to touch the reins. This is theoretically correct but it is less necessary in the case of ladies. Young riders keep themselves in their place with the help of the bridle, but there are practical difficulties to be met with when an attempt is made to deprive them of that support. If a ride consists of a good number of pupils, the most feasible plan is to let them have their snaffle reins, but to keep them at a walk till they have got a good position, and as far as possible, to prevent them from bearing heavily on the horses' mouths. Ladies are superior to men in lightness of hand, and they learn more quickly how to ride and manage a horse. Perhaps their natural kindness has its influence on these constitutionally sensitive animals. In any case, kind treatment goes a long way with the horse, and a lump or two of sugar judiciously bestowed will make him a confiding friend. It is sad to think how brutally and ungratefully he is used in this Christian country, and most brutally in his old age.

ONE WORD ON CHILDREN.

A word may be said here on the way in which children are often taught to ride, and it must be a word of warning. It is charitable to suppose that the parents of these infants do not know at what pace they are dragged at the heels of a groom who, as a rule, looks straight before him and seems to think of nobody but himself. Although the spectacle is of frequent occurrence in the Row, it has not ceased to be alarming. A child requires far more attention and supervision than an older person does; the strength of the child is much smaller than his spirit, and it is easy to cause permanent injury by overtaxing it. His riding lessons should, therefore, be given with less publicity and greater sedateness; they should also be carefully graduated so as to develop his powers and growth before fast riding in the Park is permitted.

THE TRAINING OF HORSES.

If a superior and trustworthy head be not employed to superintend the operation of breaking, the owner would find it advantageous to look after the breaker, and for this purpose some knowledge and judgment are necessary. Love of the horse is essential to success in bringing out the best qualities of the animal. This does not, however, imply that punishment is to be unknown, but that it is to be inflicted without temper, judiciously, unwillingly, and only for wilful misconduct.

When a young horse is brought up for training, the treatment which he at first receives, should depend very much on his age and past history. The general practice is to feed him almost entirely on bran mashes for the first forty-eight hours, and perhaps give a ball soon after his arrival. His exercise during the first three days should not be more than twenty minutes, morning and afternoon.

A mouthing snaffle should be used to begin with, and for the first six days he should be longed on the right rein at a walk and trot, say, twenty minutes, and on the left rein ten minutes, being occasionally allowed to come up to the trainer for rest. The trainer should stretch out his horse's forelegs when he comes up, and then make much of him and give him a piece of sliced carrot or something else that the horse likes.

The horse should be made to bend and look in the direction he takes, and the outer rein should be the higher in order to support him.

In longeing, two lessons should generally be given on the right to one on the left, as the near fore is the "mother leg," and the horse is naturally more supple on the left side.

In the second week the foregoing lessons should be repeated, and the canter be commenced, but care should be taken not to overdo it. The trainer should see that the horse canters true on each rein. He should also rein back a few paces at a time, but without putting too much weight on the haunches; and he should bend the horse to the right and left at the halt and teach him to cross his feet. These lessons should occupy from twenty to twenty-five minutes twice a day, in addition to which he ought to be walked out every day with the crosstrees, among horses and carriages in the streets, and by the end of the second week he will probably begin to show an improvement in condition. Should he not yet do so, he must be kept at the same gentle exercise for a few days longer.

The young horse must be in condition before any attempt is made to mount him. Many horses have been ruined by being mounted too soon, and by other kinds of bad management. Experience and a constant exercise of judgment are needful during the process of training. The dumb jockey is not intended, as some suppose, for a punishment, but to assist in preparing the young horse for a rider. The snaffle should be fitted with indiarubber, which preserves the delicacy of the mouth, and the two reins on each side should be leather, because with indiarubber reins the horse is apt to lean on the bit, and lower his forehand. This is an unpleasant habit, which may pull a rider off. On wet days he should stand with the trees on him in a loose box or on pillar reins, but the reins must not be too tight or he may become hard mouthed and a borer. Last of all, before mounting, it is advisable to longe the horse with the saddle, and the dumb jockey on it. This will finish the second week, or the extra days which may have been found necessary. Longeing, properly carried out, is a most useful part of a horse's education. In the case of a harness horse, trotting should predominate; in that of a riding horse, cantering.

In the third week the horse may be mounted, but most carefully in all respects. The saddle must be softly stuffed and lined, and there must be no lumps nor any substance that can possibly irritate the skin. The india-rubber snaffle should still be used, and the horse should be worked on the same circle for six days, at the walk, trot, and canter, varied by mounting and dismounting, bending, shoulder in and out, and passage. These lessons should last for thirty minutes in the morning, and twenty in the afternoon. After each of them the customary slice of carrot, or other reward for a good equine scholar, should be given, and the horse should be ridden to his stable.

At the beginning of the fourth week he may be fitted with bit complete, and be ridden anywhere, but the lessons on the circle should be repeated for ten minutes every day. The polo short cheek bit and snaffle may be recomended, with india-rubber or leather at the back of the curb.

If the horse be now ridden regularly, six days a week, until the end of the sixth week of Training, he should then have learned to obey the rider's leg, and go through all paces as required.

It is at this stage to be taken for granted that the horse knows his duty, and is willing to do it without being constantly rewarded and made much of. The coaxing treatment must, by degrees, be less frequently employed, and obedience must be gently but firmly enforced. It is very seldom that horses trained in this way turn out badly; if they do, the mischief may generally be traced to the ignorance or cruelty of some untrustworthy person. Experience teaches that there is not often any lasting cure of wild or vicious horses, by systems which involve pain and terror, but it is likewise to be borne in mind, that when a horse under training, disobeys a reasonable order which he understands, he must by all means be reduced to obedience. This is not to be done, however, in a rough or rash manner, but with quiet determination, which has the best effect both on a child and a young horse, between which there is a curious resemblance. Nothing raises the spirit of resistance either in one or the other, so much as undeserved harshness. Both may be ruined by it, but they may also be spoiled for life, if the rod is spared when it ought to be applied.

The following is Captain Nolan's catechism, which should be learned by every trainer. It is a most valuable document, now becoming very rare.

CAPTAIN NOLAN'S CATECHISM ON THE TRAINING OF HORSES.

1.—In riding a young horse at what must you first aim?
I must get him to move forward.

2.—What next?
To step out freely at a walk and a trot.

3.—Then to render him obedient, how do you begin?

With the head and neck.

4.—Why?

Because the head neck should precede or begin every movement of the horse.

5.—How do you set about it?

By teaching the horse to obey the feeling of the reins.

6.—Do you do this on foot or on horseback?

I begin with the bending lessons on foot, and thus, prepare the horse to obey the hand when mounted.

7.—What follows?

Teaching the horse to obey the pressure of the leg.

8.—How is this done?

By circling him on the forehand and haunches.

9.—Is the horse then sufficiently broken in?

No. For as yet I have only reduced, separately to obedience the head and neck, the shoulders and the haunches, one after another.

10.—To derive any great advantage from these several separate acts of obedience on the part of the horse, what must you do?

I must know how to combine them, and exact obedience from all collectively.

11.—But how can you do this?

I can bring the horse's head home, (because he has already been taught to rein in).

I can keep his hind quarters on a straight line (for by circling on the forehand, the horse has learnt to step to the right or left, from the pressure of the leg).

I can move his forehand, (from having circled on the haunches).

I therefore now proceed to rein back, and bring his loins into play.

12.— Will reining back alone, then, combine the play of forehand and haunches?

Not thoroughly without the use of the spur.

13.—Then in what way does the spur assist?

By the use of the spur I oblige the horse to bring his head and neck, shoulders, loins and haunches, all into play at the same time, and by degress I exact obedience from them collectively.

14.—Explain how this is done?

I keep the horse at a walk on the straight line, his head reined in, and approaching the spur close to the sides, touch him lightly at first. This gives the horse a forward impulse, which I quietly control by keeping my hand steady, while the horse's hind legs, which he brought under him to spring forward, are suddenly kept there by the opposition of my hand. I then make much of him and caress him, ease my hand, letting him continue to walk on quietly, till by repeating this lesson, at the slightest pressure of my legs, he brings his haunches under him, and arches his neck and is ready to spring forward, to rein back, or turn to either hand.

15.—But suppose when you stick the spurs into him, he throws up his head, and dashes off with you?

This could not happen to me because I should never communicate an impulse with the leg, which I could not control with my hand. I begin by touching his sides so lightly, and taking it so coolly, neither moving hand or leg, that the horse is never alarmed, thinks nothing of it at first, and thus I go on gradually increasing the dose, till he takes as much as is " necessary " and " cannot help himself."

16.—When do you know that the horse has taken as much as is " necessary " ?

When I feel the horse so buoyant and light under me, that I can make him spring forward, rein back, or turn to any side and with perfect ease.

17.—And how is it that he " cannot help himself" ?

Because I have made myself master, by degrees, of all his strong places, being careful to attack them one by one, and never attempt No. 2 till I was in full possession of No. 1.

18.—Then, according to your showing, you first make yourself master of the forehand, then of the haunches, and then you combine the play of both by " reining back," and using the spur. Do you now consider yourself master of your horse ?

Yes, I do.

19.—When you bend your horse to the right and left, whether on foot or mounted, is it sufficient that he should champ the bit ?

Not quite, he should open his mouth and take no hold of it.

20.—Do you continue these bending lessons long ?

Until the horse yields and opens his mouth at the slightest feeling of the reins.

21.—In " reining back " which comes first, " the pressure of the legs," or " the feeling of the reins " ?

First, the pressure of the legs, and then the feeling of the reins.

22.—Why ?

Because the support (the hind leg) must be displaced before the weight is thrown on it. If the reins are felt first the whole weight of the horse is thrown on his hind legs; and how can he lift them and step back ? If he succeeds in lifting one leg it is with a great effort, and he will *fall back* on it rather than step back, and thus injure his hocks, if *forced* to repeat it often ; whereas, by a pressure of both legs, I make him raise one hind leg, at that moment, by feeling both reins, I oblige him to put that foot down, back instead of forward. I do not throw the horse off his balance, and he can continue stepping back, with as little effort as stepping to the front.

23—Do the hand and leg work separately?

No, they should always assist each other.

24—When circling on the forehand do you ever halt the horse?

Yes, when the leg is applied, the horse moves from it, but when the pressure ceases, the horse should no longer step from it, otherwise when he once begins passaging, he is not easily stopped, and to prevent a horse getting into this bad habit, as well as to teach him to collect himself whenever the leg is applied, after each step in circling on the forehand, I stop him by closing the inward leg; and by a pressure of both legs, I collect and press him up to the hand, but I never allow him to hurry.

25.—And now how do you pull up a horse when at full speed.

By closing both legs, and feeling both reins.

26.—Do you mean to say that you pull a horse when at speed by the use of your legs.

Yes, the horse is so accustomed, at the pressure of the rider's legs, to bring his haunches under him, that he does so at speed also, and I seize that moment to keep him there by throwing myself back, feeling both reins at the same time.

27.—If you did not use your legs, what would happen?

If I did not use my legs, but merely pulled at the bridle, the horse would put his head up or down, and though I should by strength of arm pull him up in time, it would be entirely on his forehand, his nose stuck out, his hind quarters up, his loins arched, and I should be thrown up and down in the saddle in a very helpless way, and thus quite unfit to act on an emergency, as the horse would be under no control.

By the above means we can bring the horse in about two months to be generally obedient, light in hand, to carry well, to walk, trot, steadily and quickly, and always in hand, to rein back freely, and close steadily to either hand, to canter to both hands and change leg; to go about on the forehand and haunches, (*Pirouette*) and thus make him a good horse for cavalry.

Captain Nolan's system is not for troop horses only, but will likewise make a hunter, a hack, or any other horse, strong in the muscles and handy. Much must be left to the judgment of the instructor or trainer of the horse, in dividing the work into lessons, day by day. He should vary some of the lessons, according to the temper and the condition of the horses. Some are sluggish, and may require the use of the spur sooner than others, but a good trainer can bring any horse under control, that has not been spoiled by previous mismanagement.

If you cannot when mounted get your horse to do what you require, dismount, and try again, or get an assistant on foot to help. If a horse is hard to rein back or in, and rests the lower jaw against his chest, use the snaffle to raise his head, and the legs to drive him forward to the hand.

Although much of Captain Nolan's system, now substantially that pursued in the British Army, was borrowed from Mons. Baucher, the famous French trainer, yet a great part was omitted, including the more fanciful movements which were not considered necessary for cavalry. The *Pirouette* was, however, recommended by Captain

Nolan as useful for a cavalry horse. It is certainly a smart way of turning about on the haunches, and can be learned by most horses with strong hocks, but whether it is worth while to take up time in teaching it is another matter. The *Pirouette* is not merely a turn about on the haunches, but a double turn about, bringing the horse back to his original front. There are few if any conceivable circumstances in which such a movement would prove practically useful to a mounted officer or soldier. When a man on foot turns to the right about, it is because something is to be done by that change of front, but if he turns right about and again right about without a pause, it can only be for the amusement of himself or somebody else. The *demi-pirouette*, or the single turn about on the haunches, would doubtless well repay the trouble of teaching, and could not but be regarded as a most useful accomplishment.

ADVANCED TRAINING.

In proceding to the further training of the horse, it is, of course, assumed that the directions already given (pp. 19 & 20) on Saddling and Bridling have been duly followed, and that the rider is seated properly in the middle of the saddle. These matters are of greater importance now that the horse is called upon to extend his paces and make greater exertion.

To make him walk well he should for some time be collected and kept back to a rate of one mile an hour; then if allowed to increase the pace he is glad to free his shoulders, and a good walk is obtained. When trotting, the same plan should be followed to make him "trot out." Exercise of this kind gives permanent freedom of action, and improves the horse not only in walking and trotting but also in galloping and leaping. An ill-made, narrow chested young horse that put one foot in front of the other in walking, and looked as if he would fall down at every step, has been known to improve so much in shape and action as to become, in two months, a very creditable hunter. Nor is this a solitary instance. The plan adopted was to drill the horse at shoulder in and out in addition to the ordinary paces, and frequently to pull his legs to the right and left as well as to the front.

LEAPING.

The horse should be taught to leap with a leading line, or, if necessary with one on each side, and without a rider, for the first two or three lessons, but the jumps should be small and the lessons short. To be slow and sure in this business is a saving of time in the end. Some corn sacks filled with straw, and laid flat on the ground, can now be ridden over, so as gradually to get his hind quarters into good condition. A little later, a bar covered with hay or straw bands may be negociated, the sacks lying in front of the bar. The height of the bar may shortly be raised to three feet, and the sacks be placed on end leaning against it. The next step is to use hurdles with the bar, and when the horse is ready to accomplish a wider jump, two bars with hurdles or sacks of straw may be placed about twelve inches apart, and be gradually moved farther from each other as the horse increases in jumping power. For a horse finishing a course of training, and in first rate condition, the hurdles may be placed with sacks on the top, and the bars may be so fixed as to make a jump upwards of five feet high and eighteen feet long, but this should of course be arrived at by slow degrees, and under the care of an experienced and judicious trainer. A good way to give further strength and practice to a horse is to ride him over three jumps, three feet high, and ten feet apart. These buck jumps are good practice both for horses and men.

SHYING.

The chief causes of shying are fear, vice, playfulness, and defective sight. When it comes from the last, the only safe course is to get rid of the horse; he may be very useful in double harness, with blinkers on him. As to the three remaining causes, it may be stated that a good horseman, especially if he and his horse know one another, can generally manage to ride past the bogey without much trouble. He uses his legs, perhaps an armed heel, and keeps up a playful feeling of the bit, all of which help to fix the horse's attention more on himself than on the dreaded object. Should this be unavailing he must not punish but turn him about on his centre, to the right and left alternately, applying the inward leg and supporting him with the outward rein. When he has made a few turns about he should press both legs and drive the horse forward This will likely succeed on the first trial, but if not he should repeat the process until it does. If a horse has sufficient work and a good rider, he will seldom shy. A nervous rider on a shying horse is a very uncomfortable combination. A steam roller is sighted half a mile off, and the rider makes up his mind that there will be a shy; he thereupon takes hard hold of the horse's head and grips tight with his legs, in ill-disguised trepidation. This is all taken in by the quadruped, who begins to look out for the cause of alarm, and spying the steam roller, feels in duty bound to fulfil his rider's expectations. Had he been ridden boldly he might have said to himself: my rider is not afraid, why should I be? It is quite possible to get a shying horse past the object by turning his head away from it, and going past at the shoulder in. As to going close up to it, a useful lesson may thereby be given to the young horse, but it cannot do much good when he has gained experience. He can see the object perfectly well a little way off, and if kept standing there for a minute he will generally be glad to pass on quietly.

REARING.

When a horse rears he should be dealt with calmly but with great severity. Heroic remedies, such as breaking a water bottle over his head, or even striking him heavily between the ears with the butt of a whip, are worse than useless. In point of fact, they have been known, over and over again, to cause an immediate repetition of the offence. Putting shot in his ears, as some do, is shameful and punishable cruelty. If a roughrider can slip off in time to pull him back with safety, and a thorough castigation be there and then administered, the result may be beneficial. Certainly if a horse comes back he should be well punished, but it is not necessary to let him get so far. Let the rider carry a very small, slight cane, and strike him gently right and left on the ears when he tries to rear, and there will, as a rule, be no further trouble for the time being. The sound of a whip near his ears will afterwards make him lower his head. In ordinary riding, if a horse rears there is some previous indication of it, which the rider should note. He should at once get hold of his snaffle rein on the right or left, as near the ring as possible, and straighten his arm, holding the rein tight, the rein on the opposite side being held normally. If this be properly done, it bends the horse's head to the right, or to the left as the case may be, and he is unable to rise because his weight is pulled to one side. If, after all, he succeeds in rearing, and is about to fall back, the rider must pull the reins on the right or left, and jump off *on the same side*. That gives the best chance of falling clear. A lady on an ordinary side saddle should always pull the near reins in these circumstances, but it is not to be supposed that a lady will ride a rearer, so nothing more need be said on the subject. The vice of rearing is so disagreeable and dangerous that the horse addicted to it should be put in a pair horse van, or between the poles of a three horse abreast omnibus.

SADDLES.

The all-important part of the saddle is the tree. If the tree fits the back of the horse, the weight of the rider is equally and fairly distributed, but if not it falls unevenly and produces a sore back. Although, as already remarked, it is not often convenient to have a saddle made for every riding horse, yet when it can be done, the resulting advantage is very decided. The owner of a very valuable riding horse should, if possible, get a tree to fit his horse, especially if the animal is to be much ridden. In other cases, and when nothing but light work is to be done, it is possible to obviate injury by stuffing the saddle so as to make it a tolerable fit, but the stuffing of saddles and collars should be minutely examined, as, owing to accident or carelessness, hard foreign matter has often found its way into stuffing, and has been the means of disabling horses. It should likewise be clearly apprehended that the blade bones and the loins are not intended to bear weight, and that if the side-boards of the tree be long enough to extend to them, the horse will sooner or later be crippled. Neither is the spine capable of bearing weight.

The following extract from Professor Smith's "Military Manual of Saddles and Sore Backs," should be studied by all who are not already familar with the structure of the part on which the saddle rests :—

"Coming out at almost right angles to the spine we have the ribs. Now as it is indirectly on the ribs that we actually sit, it is essential that we should have some knowledge of the part. The ribs form a case called the chest. This case is narrow in front and wide behind. The ribs in front, those situated under the fore leg, are short, straight, wide, and fixed both above and below; as, however, we pass backwards we find they become more arched, narrow, and flexible. This arching of the back ribs produces a very remarkable change in size which can only be appreciated by looking down on a horse as he is led past you with nothing on his back. In no position can it be better seen than from a driver's seat of a London omnibus, as the horses which work in these wear no other harness than collar and traces, and the back is exposed to full view. I can assure you that a study from this position is of inestimable benefit in learning how a back works, but more particularly in obtaining a correct appreciation of a point I have to deal with presently, viz., the movements performed by the shoulder blade.

"If a section of a horse's body be made immediately behind the play of his shoulder, we find that the part is here egg-shaped, whilst if we cut him through behind the last rib the body is nearly circular in shape; this difference in shape is due to the arrangement of the ribs as before described. If we look carefully at the ribs, and I will only direct your attention to the last 11, we find that those behind the play of the shoulder are wide, comparatively straight, and attached to the breast bone, which affords them great support; their upper surface which forms the back is narrow; as, however, we pass backwards we find that the ribs present a gradually increasing width of upper surface; the difference between the upper level surface of the ribs behind the shoulder and that in front of the loin being as much as three inches in favour of the latter. On the width of these level surfaces depends the width of the back, and on them rest indirectly the side-boards of the saddle."

When once these principles have been grasped, in addition to that already laid down, that the rider should sit in the middle of the saddle, it will not be difficult to detect anything faulty either in the construction or the fitting of that very important article.

A new side-saddle should be used for a fortnight before the owner rides in it, in order to avoid the trouble that may arise from finding out something wrong when she is on horseback. Special care should be taken in the fitting of the saddle on the off side, where the horse often becomes tender and saddle sore from the extra strain of the rider's weight on that side. Her balance-strap should not be attached to the stirrup, as the girth bulk of the horse decreases after riding for some time, and the stirrup becomes too long.

The ladies of officers' families, and others going abroad, are recommended to take their saddles with them. They are likely to be much better satisfied if they do so, and should they cease to require them, they will rarely fail to obtain a good price for English saddles.

DRIVING.

Before a horse can be considered properly broken to harness, he should have been put through the foregoing course of training,

including longeing, riding, and the aids
Nothing fits a horse so well for his harness
work, as being intelligently trained on the
system above described. The next point
to be considered is the fitting of the
harness. What is often called vice and
temper, is merely the result of intense
irritation or pain caused by ill-fitting
harness. A tightly buckled crupper, may
so rub and injure a horse's dock, that he
kicks a carriage to pieces. His shoulders
may be so tender from excessive collar work
at the beginning of his training, that he
becomes a jibber. The object of these few
words under the head of DRIVING, is to
mitigate the hardships both of the horse
and his master. The horse must be trained
step by step, and each step should be
firmly planted before the next is taken.
After passing through the training detailed
above, he should stand in the stable on
pillar reins for a few days, with the harness
on, and champ the bit. He may then be
led out, one man being at his head and
another holding on to a rope attached to
the traces. The man pulling at the traces,
gets the horse by degrees to pull against
him, and so draw him along. The man at

the horse's head then changes his position, drives him from behind, and turns him to the right and left. After this he may be put in a brake with a steady old horse, getting light work, and being rewarded with sugar or carrot, and when his shoulders become hard as they will do under this management, he will take very kindly to his harness duties.

The general principles on which the harness should be fitted can be gathered from the passages on SADDLING AND BRIDLING, (pp. 19 & 20) The pad should be behind the play of the shoulder, the crupper should admit the breadth of a hand between it and the hind quarters, a few inches in front of the tail, the collar should fit easily, allowing the hand to pass freely between the lower part of it and the horse's chest, and there should as a rule be NO BEARING REIN. A well made horse, in good condition, and properly treated, carries his head in a natural position, and is both pained and disfigured by having such an addition to his outfit. The unnatural position produced by the bearing rein, may hide defects, but it is at the expense of the animal's sufferings.

With regard to the driving itself, it seems to deteriorate in this country, probably from the fact that nowadays more people keep carriages than formerly, many of them uninterested in horses, and unable to give proper directions to their servants, while the latter, from want of supervision, frequently remain untutored, or become careless.

There are several rules which should be invariably followed by coachmen. They should sit with their feet well in front of them and so be ready to recover a horse if he stumbles rather than be pulled off the box by him. Nothing more surely indicates a bad driver than the position with feet drawn back instead of planted forward. The reins should not be either slack or tight but should preserve a sympathetic feeling of the mouth, by which the horse is kept in touch with the wish and intention of the driver. The whip should be used sparingly, and more as an aid than as a punishment. Never start suddenly.

Never race; it is a far superior line of conduct to let people pass you on the road than to compete with them. Their business may be urgent, in which case they are right, but if they wish to get ahead of you merely for the sake of doing so, still maintain your own pace and make no sign but pull aside and let them pass. If a snob pushes to enter a doorway in front of you, it is generally better to stand off and let him have his way. What he does shows what he is. The driver who thinks it meritorious to pass you on the road, makes a similar mistake. Owners should see that their servants act on this principle, whatever kind of carriage they may be driving. Never, except on rare and urgent occasions, speak to horses when driving in a town, and never on any occasion in a loud voice.

If a horse persists in cantering, whether in single or double harness, make sure that the curb is not too tight or the leverage excessive from the too low buckling of the reins. These points may on examination be found all right, and yet something may press on him on one side or the other, making him lead off with a particular foot. When all known causes have been removed, and he still persists in cantering, pull his head quietly away from the leading leg, and touch him very gently on the opposite side with the whip. This will oblige him to change feet and he will then probably trot. The ignorant and futile attempts made to stop cantering in harness tend to show the advisability of giving systematic instruction to men who have the care of horses.

Then under the head of over-driving and neglect, there is room for vast improvement. The pace, the distance driven, the times of rest and feeding, the refreshment of meal and water, and the attention to the animal's general well-being, can only be properly regulated by the knowledge and kind feeling of the person who takes charge, and no one who is not possessed of these two requisites should ever be entrusted with horses.

One word may be said on the turn-out and attitude of men on the box of a private carriage in the street. They should always be well set up, neatly and correctly dressed, their hats never on one side, the arms of the footman folded; they should look straight to the front, and never speak to each other except on duty. In short, their demeanour should be that of soldiers at attention. If the horses, carriage, and harness, correspond with the above description, the owner and coachman will everywhere deserve and receive respect, but opposite causes produce opposite effects.

STABLES AND OTHER SUBJECTS.

A stable should be dry, well ventilated, free from draughts, fairly warm, and contain sufficient cubic space. It will not be dry unless it is well drained. There should be no sunk drains to go wrong and poison the air that the horses breathe. All the drains, should, if possible, be shallow, and on the surface, thus admitting of being thoroughly cleaned and flushed, and preventing the accumulation of unseen decomposing matter. The effect of pure air on the health of a horse is as great as on that of a human being, and no horse can long be in good health if kept in a damp and close stable. The breathing space in nearly all the newest and best stables, is 1500 cubic feet and upwards for each horse.

The paving material, in order to be sanitary, must be impervious to moisture. This likewise applies to the walls, which should be faced with glazed tiles or some other sanitary material. Horses should stand on level ground, and therefore the stalls should be made level. In new stables this would probably be the case, but when one is in possesion of a stable with sloping stalls, the following plan may be adopted: Completely cover the floor of the stall with a level platform of thick planks raised very slightly off the ground; the planks must be bored with a sufficient number of auger holes to let water run through. Very little bedding is needed in such stalls, and in fact, vast numbers of horses sleep comfortably on wood, without any bedding whatever. But scrupulous and regular cleanliness is absolutely necessary; the planks ought to be taken up and cleaned daily, and the pavement beneath them carefully washed and dried. In ordinary cases however, there should be an ample allowance of good clean straw for the horse's bed. Eight pounds of fresh straw every day may be considered a fair average, that quantity being prescribed for military stables.

For full information on these matters, "Horses and Stables," by Sir F. Fitz-

Wygram, may be consulted. It is an exhaustive work, and is sold at a very low price, which brings it within the reach of all.

SHOEING, AND THE STRUCTURE OF THE FOOT, are subjects too large for discussion here.

The FEEDING of the horse cannot be duly regulated except by the amount of work which he does. The cavalry ration of oats is ten pounds a day, which is generally sufficient, but horses in hard work require more. The oats should be home grown, not too new, not artificially dried, and should weigh nearly forty pounds to the bushel. It is more economical to buy good and expensive oats than the cheaper sorts.

Hay for horses doing ordinary fast work, must be "upland," fragrant, and well saved. Other *desiderata* are that it should be free from dust, composed of a variety of good grasses, and be about a year old. A fair average amount of hay is twelve pounds a day for each horse. Green forage and other kinds of food, may be given occasionally as circumstances and the judgment of the owner suggest.

Water should be soft, clean, and, if very cold, should be chilled. It should be given before feeding and not after.

GROOMING should be thoroughly, energetically, and regularly done, for otherwise neither the horse's general health nor the gloss on his coat will be satisfactory.

DOCKING is a cruel and brutal fashion, which all who appreciate the horse, and understand his constitution, would be glad to see unmistakeably abolished by law. The reader may be referred for details, and for an able presentment on Docking, to a book recently published under the sanction of the Royal Society for the Prevention of Cruelty to Animals, entitled "The Wanton Mutilation of Animals," by the celebrated Dr. Fleming, lately at the head of the Veterinary Department of the Army. He says that it is "painful and unnecessary," damages the animal for life, and brings those who practise it within the scope of the law for the prevention of cruelty to animals.

Dr. Fleming quotes Voltaire, whose disgust with the unnatural appearance of our horses, impelled him to write the following lines;—

> "Vous fiers Anglois,
>   Barbares que vous êtes,
>   Coupez la tête aux rois
>   Et la queue à vos bêtes;
>   Mais les François,
>   Polis et droits,
>   Aimant les lois,
>   Laissent la queue aux bêtes
>   Et la tête à leurs rois."

This may be roughly translated thus:—
  You English are not only haughty,
  But also barbarous and naughty,
  For head of king and tail of horse,
  You amputate without remorse.
  The French are, *au contraire*, polite,
  Abide the law, and love the right,
  Keep horses' tails as they have grown,
  And leave their Monarchs' heads alone.

Afterwards the French followed our example by committing both of the sins condemned by Voltaire, but if we desire to be in the van of civilization we should try to reclaim those whom we have led astray, and our first step must be to abandon our evil ways with shame and contrition.

THOMAS & SONS,

HUNTING OUTFITTERS, SPORTING TAILORS, and BREECHES MAKERS.

Hunting and Cubbing Coats and Breeches of Superior Cut and Finish.

THOMAS & SONS' PATENT WASHABLE WATERPROOF SKIRT LININGS FOR HUNTING COATS.

A great boon to hunting men. Hunting Coats fitted with it last twice as long, and require one-half the amount of cleaning.

CAVALRY PANTALOONS AND OVERALLS A SPECIALITY.

THOMAS & SONS,
Sporting and Military Tailors and Breeches Makers,
32, BROOK STREET, W.
(Corner of South Molton Street).

TELEGRAPHIC ADDRESS: "SPORTINGLY, LONDON."

SADDLES & BRIDLES.

Mr. Savigear has made special terms with a large Wholesale Manufacturer of Ladies' and Gentlemen's saddles of the **very best quality.**

(A LARGE REDUCTION).

It is most essential that Ladies should be properly fitted with their side saddle for comfort and a firm seat.

SPECIALLY MADE SADDLES & BRIDLES,

With Solid Nickel Bits.

(For India and the Colonies, &c.—To fit any horse).

SAVIGEAR'S RIDING GRIP TEST.

No rider should be without one. It proves the strength of seat, and number of pounds you can hold on the saddle with your knees. Also the pulling strength on ladies' saddle, and the number of pounds she can pull on the horse's mouth.

22/6 complete.

APPLY:—

SAVIGEAR'S RIDING SCHOOL.

SPINK BROS.,

𝔅utchers,

Earl's Court, S.W.
AND AT
Marylebone
Cricklewood & Paddington.

Specialities

| SCOTCH BEEF. | NEW ZEALAND LAMB. |
| SCOTCH MUTTON. | NEW ZEALAND MUTTON. |

SPECIALLY SELECTED.

Dairy Fed Pork.   West Country Veal.
Sweetbreads.   Calves' Heads.   Calves' Feet.

Families waited on daily for Orders.

STORE PRICES.

EARLY DELIVERIES TO ALL PARTS OF LONDON.

Price Lists on Application.

SPINK BROS.,
𝔈arl's 𝔈ourt.

W. WAY, R.S.S., JUDGE OF SHOEING TO THE SOMERSET COUNTY AGRICULTURAL ASSOCIATION, 1897-8.

Shoeing Forges,

1a, WALLGRAVE ROAD,
AND
8, CHILDS PLACE, EARLS COURT, S.W.

W. POPE & SON, Veterinary Surgeons.

Hunters & Ladies' Hacks Shod on the latest & approved principles.

W. GOULT,

Hosier, Hatter and Umbrella Manufacturer.

DRESS SHIRTS, TIES AND GLOVES.

Hats Ironed and Umbrellas Repaired and Re-covered while waiting.

169, EARLS COURT ROAD,

Opposite Railway Station.

W. H. VERLANDER,
Saddler and Harness Maker,
AND Horse Clothing Manufacturer.

HORSES CAREFULLY MEASURED AND FITTED.   ALL STABLE REQUISITES.
Portmanteaus neatly and thoroughly Repaired.
CONTRACTS TAKEN.   ESTIMATES GIVEN FREE.

95, MUNSTER ROAD, FULHAM.

NATIVE OYSTERS.

F. SAVAGE,

3, Prince Teck Buildings,

EARL'S COURT.

WENHAM LAKE ICE.

FISH, POULTRY AND GAME.

Always a large selection of the finest Poultry and Game.

FAMILIES WAITED ON DAILY.

The Favour of your Patronage is respectfully solicited.

Invaluable to Sportsmen.

Used by Lady and Gentlemen Riders. Jockeys, Athletes, etc.

REDUCTION OF CORPULENCY without dieting or drugs: without danger or discomfort. Amiral Soap reduces fat from that part of the body to which it is applied. Of all Chemists, or by sending Postal Orders for 8/- to The Figure Improving Soap Company, Limited, 3, Throgmorton Avenue, London, E.C. Pamphlets, etc., post free on application.

THE EARLS COURT BOOT STORES,
128b, Earls Court Road.

Makers of Ladies' and Gentlemen's Riding and Walking Boots.

——— ALSO ———

Makers of the Special "Silent" House Shoe, Price only 3/11

THREE DOORS FROM FOPSTONE ROAD.

FARMER & SONS,
Printers & Stationers, Military & General Booksellers,

Supply everything required by Military & other Students on the most favourable terms.

36, HIGH STREET AND 1, EDWARDES TERRACE, KENSINGTON.

WORKS: 295, EDGWARE ROAD, LONDON, W.

OFFORD AND SONS,

Coachbuilders & Harness Makers,

92 & 94 GLOUCESTER ROAD, SOUTH KENSINGTON

AND AT

30 Fulham Rd., S.W. & 67 George St., W.

NEW AND SECOND-HAND CARRIAGES.

REPAIRS. HIRE. INSURANCE.

OFFORD'S "CHARETTE," Regd.

The Newest and most elegant Panel Car.   Easiest of access.   Perfect in finish.   Price from **35** Guineas.

Drags, Phaetons, Carts and every class of Carriages on Sale or Hire.

Telephone Nos. 809 KENSINGTON, 5118 GERARD.   Telegraphic Address: HAYSTACKS, LONDON.

HOOD & MOORE'S STORES,
LIMITED,

Hay & Straw Salesmen, and Corn Merchants,

FOREIGN HAY AND MOSS LITTER IMPORTERS,

63 NEW CORN EXCHANGE, MARK LANE,
E.C.

Wholesale Depots—

Shepherd's Bush Wharf, L. & N.W. Railway,
Greyhound Wharf, Crab Tree, Fulham,

AND ELSEWHERE.

Counting House—6, SHEPHERD'S BUSH GREEN. W.

R. G. CALLABY & SON'S
Riding Establishments,

DULWICH WOOD HOUSE, SYDENHAM HILL, AND HUNSTANTON.

HORSES BOUGHT AND SOLD ON COMMISSION.

Riding Master—
HORACE CALLABY.   **Breeders of Horses.**

ARTHUR PERRIN, OF THE DORKING COACH.
"HARE & HOUNDS," East Sheen.
Three minutes from Mortlake Station.
Bowling Green and Good Stabling.

The London Anti-Vivisection Society,

32, Sackville Street, Piccadilly, London, W.

Founded 1876 for the suppression of the Scientific Torture of Animals.

"**Heartily sympathising with your efforts.**"—*Extract from a letter from H.M. the Queen to the Secretary of this Society.*

Lord Shaftesbury.—"Vivisection is an abominable sin."
Lord Brampton.—"I abominate vivisection; should rejoice to see it legally suppressed."
Sir Henry Irving —"Fully in sympathy."

PATRONS:

The Duke of Portland
The Dowager Countess of Kintore
The Dowager Duchess of Manchester
The Dowager Marchioness of Ormonde
The Countess of Lindsey
The Earl of Lindsay
The Countess of Lindsay
The Countess of Dundonald
The Countess of Roden
The Countess of Norbury
The Countess of Munster
Lord Ernest Hamilton

Lord Llangattock
Lord Hatherton, C.M.G.
Lord Leigh
Lord Robartes
The Bishop of Argyle and the Isles
The Archbishop of Ontario
Bishop Hellmuth
Lord Brampton
Canon Wilberforce
Rev. Preb. Webb-Peploe
James Sant, Esq., R.A.

MEDICAL PATRONS:

Surgeon-General Sir Charles Gordon, K.C.B., M.D. (Hon. Physician to H.M. the Queen).
Surgeon-General J. H. Thornton, C.B., B.A., M.B.
Surgeon-General Watson, M.D.
A. Wall, Esq., M.R.C.S., L.R.C.P.
A. J. H. Crespi, Esq. (Hertford Coll., Oxon), M.R.C.P. (Medallist in Surgery).
A. A. Beale, Esq., M.B., C.M.
T. G. Vawdrey, Esq., L.R.C.P., M.R.C.S.
Stephen F. Smith, Esq., L.S.A.
R. M. Bowstead, Esq., M.D., M.R.C.S.
G. Herbert Lilley, M.D., M.R.C.P., M.R.C.S.

Professor Lawson Tait, F.R.C.S., M.D., L.L.D.
John Clarke, Esq., M.D., M.B.
Stephen Townesend, Esq., F.R.C.S.
F. Cann, Esq., F.R.C.S.
The Rev. Francis Smith, M.A., M.D., M.R.C.S.
Ed. Haughton, B.A., M.D., M.R.C.S.
F. S. Arnold, Esq., B.A., Oxon., M.B., M.R.C.S.
Hector Munro, Esq., M.B., C.M.
F. E. Vernede, Esq., L.R.C.P., M.R.C.S.
Walter R. Hadwen, Esq., M.D., etc.

The Annual Report and Literature free on Application.

The Committee most earnestly appeal for aid to enable them to carry on a more Vigorous Campaign.

OFFICES: 32, SACKVILLE STREET, PICCADILLY, LONDON, W.

Hon. Sec.:—Mrs. F. C. JAMES.   Secretary:—SIDNEY G. TRIST, Esq.
Treasurer:—Dr. WALL.

Royal Society  for the
PREVENTION OF CRUELTY TO ANIMALS

Patrons.
HER MOST GRACIOUS MAJESTY THE QUEEN.
THEIR ROYAL HIGHNESSES THE PRINCE AND PRINCESS OF WALES.

President.
HIS ROYAL HIGHNESS THE DUKE OF YORK, K.G.

UPON this Institution, founded in 1824 (the only one having for its object the protection of sentient and defenceless animals), rests a heavy responsibility. It is earnestly and respectfully submitted, that it has in consequence a strong claim upon the benevolence of the humane and charitable.

OBJECTS.

The inculcation of the duty of Justice, Kindness, and Mercy to God's Dumb and Defenceless Creatures, by means of sermons, lectures, addresses, &c., in churches, chapels, schools, public meetings; by articles in newspapers; by the publication of monthly illustrated journals; by the preparation of nearly 200 different books, pamphlets, leaflets, for general circulation; obtaining improvements in the law protecting animals by administration of the existing statutes against cruelty; by issuing placards broadcast warning persons against the commission of offences; by the establishment of branches and auxiliaries throughout the country (upwards of 200 of which are already in active union); by the employment of officers in uniform or otherwise, nearly 150 of whom are engaged to watch the conduct of cruel persons in the streets, in slaughter-houses, in mines, on canal banks, on highways, at markets and fairs, during transit of animals on railway trucks, steamships, and in all places where their services are usefully employed; by juvenile societies called Bands of Mercy (more than 1,000 of which have been formed in the villages and towns of the United Kingdom), &c.

EDUCATION COMMITTEE.—An Education Committee has been established for the preparation of Literature, the circulation of Papers among persons entrusted with Cattle, such as Coachmen, Carters, and Drovers; for the introduction into Schools of Books and Teaching calculated to impress on Youth the duty of humanity towards the inferior animals; for making ethical and persuasive appeals to the public through the Press, and otherwise awakening public opinion; and for obtaining the delivery of Discourses from the Pulpit, &c.

SERMONS.—On the Fourth Sunday after Trinity Clergymen are cordially and kindly asked to respond to the Society's invitation to preach sermons on 'Man's Duty to God's Dumb, Defenceless Creatures, and it is hoped these sermons will be annually.

LECTURES.—Many hundreds of lectures on the proper treatment of animals, &c., are delivered annually in Public Halls, in Institutes, in Schools, at Band of Hope Meetings, &c., the object of which is to promote kindness and prevent cruelty.

BANDS OF MERCY have been formed in hundreds of parishes for the training of children and young persons in habits of mercy at meetings regularly held by local managers. (A pamphlet, entitled 'Information,' may be had gratis on application to the undersigned.)

BRANCHES have been established in most of the large towns of England.

The increased operations of the Society have drawn from the funds an amount vastly exceeding the yearly subscriptions. The Committee need much greater assistance, and unless such additional support be extended to them, this most righteous cause of humanity must suffer from insufficiency of means to carry out those many urgent measures which every well-wisher of the Society has so deeply at heart. Remittances may be forwarded to

105 Jermyn Street, London. **JOHN COLAM,** *Secretary.*

SUPPORTED ONLY BY VOLUNTARY CONTRIBUTIONS.

FORM OF BEQUEST.

In benefactions by will to this Society, which being well established is not likely to die, it is important to use the following form:

'I give and bequeath   to be paid to the Treasurer for the time being of the ROYAL SOCIETY FOR THE PREVENTION OF CRUELTY TO ANIMALS, established 1824, to be at the disposal of the Committee for the time being of the said Society, and I direct that the same be paid free of legacy duty.'

SYDNEY R. SMITH
Sporting Books
Canaan, New York 12029

www.ingramcontent.com/pod-product-compliance
Lightning Source LLC
Chambersburg PA
CBHW022130160426
43197CB00009B/1228